Maddalena archipelago Join a cruise at Palau to experience the sublime beauty of this island chain *(page 64)*

Grotta di Nettuno Visit the island's most spectacular cave *(page 71)*

Golfo di Orosei This lovely stretch of coast is best seen from the water *(page 57)*

Carloforte The pretty port makes a good base for exploring the coast of the island of San Pietro *(page 37)*

Bosa Narrow streets lead through the picturesque old town *(page 72)*

Alghero Sardinian life unfolds at a relaxed pace on the streets and squares of Alghero's Historic Centre *(page 68)*

CONTENTS

24

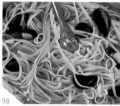

98

44

INTRODUCTION

In 1921, when D.H. Lawrence decided he needed a break from his home in Sicily, he opted for an island 'outside the circuit of civilisation'. After an abundance of culture in Sicily and other parts of Italy, he was seeking a place of simplicity, or, as he described Sardinia, 'belonging to nowhere'.

Over 80 years on, Sardinia still feels quite distinct from the rest of Italy. In common with other Mediterranean islands it has been occupied, colonised and exploited by successive waves of invaders. Few of these powers saw it as anything more than a useful trading post at the crossroads of crucial Mediterranean sea routes. The Phoenicians plundered it for the rich ore deposits in the west, the Romans exploited it for grain, otherwise regarding it as an unhealthy backwater, the Spaniards treated it as a remote European outpost; Nelson coveted the island as a naval base, but failed to persuade the British to buy it. While other Mediterranean islands have adopted the character of their colonisers – Malta becoming British, Crete Greek, the Ballearics Spanish just to name a few – Sardinia has retained a remarkable cultural identity. It may not have the sophistication or the wealth of sights that greet you in Sicily or cities on the mainland, but it is a land which is truly steeped in tradition and custom. Local dialects still thrive, artisan skills have been revived and religious and pagan traditions are celebrated by more than 1,000 annual festivals. Moreover each region retains its culinary specialities, from elaborate home-made bread and pastries to suckling pig slowly roasted and served on a bed of myrtle leaves.

Columns from the Roman temple at the ancient city of Tharros on the Sinis Peninsula

Tourism Today

Much of course has changed since Lawrence's day. Since the 1960s the international jetset have been flocking to the Costa Smeralda, mere mortals to less famous resorts on low-cost airlines. Brochure descriptions of Sardinia as 'a slice of the Seychelles' or 'Italy's Caribbean' are not complete hyperbole. It would be hard to find a concentration of such enticing beaches anywhere else in the Mediterranean. The sands are white, the waters come in every conceivable shade of blue and green and the wind-sculpted rocks, cliffs, dunes and marshes provide stunning and continually shifting vistas. The island has 1,800km (1,125 miles) of shoreline which is a quarter of the entire Italian seaboard. The chiselled nature of the coast, with its rocky inlets, bays and promontories, accounts for this surprisingly high figure. Sheer cliffs and lack of access have largely precluded heavy development and though recent years have seen self-catering complexes sprouting on hills behind, large tracts of the shore are still almost untouched. Some beaches, like Chia in the south and Piscinas in the southwest stretch for miles. Moreover Sardinia boasts 300 sunny days a year and reliably hot, dry and sunny weather from May to September. The short-lived holiday season, from June to early September, is gradually extending into late spring and early autumn, particularly for hikers, bikers and others who want to explore the island without the crowds. In winter coastal resorts close down with the exception of Alghero, which (now served by Ryanair from three different UK airports) is lively all year round.

Beach bliss

In the high season (late June to early September) space on the easily accessible beaches is at a premium; but travellers who are prepared to negotiate unsigned dirt tracks or scramble down steep paths are likely to find space in secluded coves.

The port of La Maddalena

The island is a haven for water sports enthusiasts. The offshore breezes, particularly in the north, provide perfect conditions for sailing and windsurfing and the translucent waters that wash the shores have given rise to numerous diving centres all around the island. Many resorts are launching pads for boat trips to explore coves, inlets, islands and otherwise inaccessible beaches.

Since most visitors escape to Sardinia for beaches or sporting activities, the cultural attractions are rarely crowded. The most abundant and distinctive of the island's monuments are the *nuraghi*, or stone towers, dating from the Bronze Age. These mysterious megaliths, built as dwellings, fortifications and sanctuaries, offer a tantalising glimpse of this early civilisation. The architectural legacy from later Mediterranean occupiers lies scattered around the island: Carthaginian and Roman remains, Pisan-Romanesque churches and Spanish-style dwellings and monuments.

Sardinia is the second largest island in the Mediterranean (after Sicily) and many tourists, daunted by its size, stay put in one resort. Main roads however are surprisingly fast and it would be a pity to miss out on a foray into the mountainous interior, a visit to one of the historic town centres or a day's merrymaking at one of the many festivals. Among the most flamboyant of Sardinia's celebrations are the Sa Sartiglia, a medieval procession and tournament at Oristano and the S'Ardia at Sédilo, featuring frenetic horseracing, not unlike that of Siena's Palio.

Flora, Fauna and the Interior

The population of the island is 1.6 million, with sheep outnumbering Sards by three to one. Inland the impression is one of emptiness and space. What was once thick woodland is now pungent *macchia*, a mixed vegetation of myrtle, juniper, arbutus, broom and cistus which presents a riot of colour in spring. The varied landscape provides habitats for some rare species including mouflon, the wild long-horned sheep, the small Sardinian deer *(cervo sardo)* and the *cavallini*, the miniature wild horses that roam on the Giara di Gésturi plain. More conspicuous and highly exotic are the large flocks of pink flamingoes seen on the lagoons of Oristano and Cágliari.

Where sheep and goats outnumber people

The landscape is rarely dramatic but the wild Gennargentu mountains in the heart of the island provide scenic hiking, trekking and rock-climbing. Isolated villages,

Locals in Orgósolo

previously the home of shepherds and bandits, are slowly opening to tourism, offering guided treks, archaeological tours and other rural diversions. While formerly most of the tourist accommodation was located on the coast there is now a large choice of *agriturismi* (farm properties) or Bed and Breakfasts for those who want a taste of rural life. It is inland that you will find the typical Sard. Over the centuries invaders who settled on the shores forced the coastal dwellers to migrate inland and raise livestock for a living. Shaped by centuries of foreign domination, the inhabitants of the rural villages, particularly in Nuoro province, are fiercely proud with a passion for freedom and independence. Indeed, most islanders regard themselves as Sardinians first, and Italians very much second. In the mountain villages where life has changed little for centuries, or is only just beginning to do so, the locals are noticeably more insular and less ebullient than the typical Italian. But like all Sards, they are generous and welcoming to visitors.

Where to Go

In the island's south, the capital, Cágliari, is well worth visiting for sightseeing, shopping and restaurants, but with its traffic-filled streets and lack of attractive hotels, it's not ideal as a holiday base. The south of the island has splendid beaches at Villasimius, along the Costa Rei and the Costa Verde, while for sightseers there are the ancient Carthaginian/Roman remains of Nora, the famous *nuraghe* of Su Nuraxi, the Spanish town of Iglesias and the offshore islands of San Pietro and Sant'Antióco. But the vast majority of foreigners favour the north of the

Marina quarter in Cágliari

island, which has the more attractive towns such as Alghero, Bosa and Castelsardo, excellent beaches and well-equipped resorts. There is also the attraction of boat trips to the Maddalena Archipelago and day cruises to the islands of Asinara, or Corsica 11km (7 miles) across the Straits of Bonifacio. In the northeast the Costa Smeralda (Emerald Coast) was developed in the 1960s as a millionaires' playground. This thin strip of coast boasts exclusive rustic-style hotels, 'private' beaches and luxury marinas. Further south, the east coast has stunning beaches, many of which are only accessible by boat from Cala Gonone. On the west of the island, Oristano's coast has no nearby international airport, so for the time being at least, remains unspoilt.

A BRIEF HISTORY

Sardinia's strategic maritime setting between Africa, Spain and Italy has always played a crucial role in the island's history. Over the centuries the island suffered the rampages of a succession of foreign invaders: Phoenicians, Carthaginians, Romans, Vandals, Pisans, Genoese and Spaniards. Each new arrival made its mark on the island, but the richest legacy was left by settlers from the dawn of history.

Early Settlers

Mystery surrounds the origins of the first settlers on the island, but evidence suggests tribes from the Italian mainland or North Africa were inhabiting caves around 6000BC. By the 4th millennium BC settlers were creating villages of circular wood huts on stone foundations. Elaborate rock-cut tombs, known as *domus de janas* ('fairy houses') date from this era, and from these evolved the *tombe di gigante* (giants' tombs), burial chambers fronted by a huge carved stele. Construction techniques of dwellings gradually developed and culminated in the evocative *nuraghi*. Dating from 1800BC–900BC, these coni-

Nuraghe Santu Antine

cal roofed towers were built with large blocks of stone without the use of mortar. Some 7,000 survive on the island, varying greatly in function and complexity. The majority are simple and compact, others such as Santu Antine at Torralba and Su Nuraxi at Barumini stand three storeys high and appear to have been fortresses, with watchtowers, bastions and other defences. Bronze statuettes unearthed at nuraghic villages offer a glimpse of a layered and complex society of aristocrats, warriors, shepherds and farmers. Sadly there is no written record from this mysterious era, but given that some of the names of the *nuraghi* have no Greek, Punic or Latin origin, the well-known expression *'il vero Sardo'* (the true Sardinian) may connote a true ethnic survival.

The first recorded settlers on the island, around 800BC, were the Phoenicians, who traded extensively in metals and established coastal settlements in the south and west. Threatened by local rebellions they appealed to the Carthaginians who gradually appropriated the coasts of the island. The most conspicuous legacy of Punic rule are the ruins of the ancient cities of Nora, Tharros and Sulcis (present-day Sant'Antióco).

Roman baths at Fordongianus

Rome and the Aftermath

Victory over Carthage in the Punic Wars led to Rome's brutal 700-year rule of Sardinia. In 227BC the island became Rome's second province, along with Corsica. In the first century or so, rebellions were quelled and after a particularly sharp revolt in 176BC many of the islanders were deported as slaves by the Romans. By 46BC Cágliari had become an important port of the Roman fleet. The islanders adopted the Latin language but the Roman remains on the island (and notably the amphitheatre at Cágliari, the ancient city of Nora and the Roman

Island backwater

The island of Sardinia was regarded by the Roman administration as an unhealthy backwater, exemplified by an act of the Emperor Tiberius who conscripted 4,000 Jewish freedmen to service there.

colony at Porto Torres) speak more to the might of the Empire and the wealth of its own expatriates than to any lasting beneficial influence on the islanders.

With the final collapse of the Roman Empire in the west, Sardinia, along with other Mediterranean islands and the whole of Roman North Africa, became a victim of barbarian raids. Vandal rule lasted until AD534, by which time Western Europe was fragmented into motley barbarian states. The most civilised European power was the surviving Roman Empire in the east, or the Byzantine Empire, which then theoretically held sway over Sardinia and other distant western outposts. But in the early 700s, during the massive surge of Islam following the death of Mohammed, great armies of Saracens (Arab Muslims) streamed across North Africa and into the Iberian Peninsula. There was little or no Christian resistance; in 711 Cágliari was sacked and occupied, and for the next two centuries the island suffered repeated Arab invasions.

Christian Influence

Despite the ongoing Arab incursions, it was in the 9th century that records first made mention of a '*giudice*' or governing judge of the land. By the early 11th century the island was divided into four *guidicati* or states: Cágliari, Arborea,

Gallura and Torres, each controlled by its own *guidice*. The system was the greatest legacy of Byzantium, which was renowned for its legal and bureaucratic administration. But by this time the papacy, along with the Holy Roman Empire, had itself become a political power. Genoa and Pisa, the two rival dominant Italian maritime powers in the western basin of the Mediterranean, were given papal permission to recover lands from the infidel. Hence Pisa captured Sardinia from the Muslims in 1016, as part of a Christian regeneration in southern Europe. Pisan occupation of the island is graphically illustrated by military architecture, and notably the medieval fortifications in the old quarter of Cágliari. The next 200 years or so were characterised by

Eleonora d'Arborea

The warrior Queen of Arborea was one of the most significant law-makers of medieval Europe. She is best known for the famous *Carta de Logu*, which was adopted as the basis for the whole island's legal code. Initiated by her father, the *giudice* Mariano IV, but promulgated during Eleonora's reign in 1392, the code consisted of 198 chapters and regulated matters as varied as crime, civil wrongs and the legal position of women, children and slaves. In 1421 this remarkably progressive code was adopted by the Aragonese rulers and remained the bedrock of the island's law until the 19th century. Eleonora was also renowned for her remarkable skill and energy in defending the independence of Arborea from Aragonese control. Married to a Genoese aristocrat of the Doria family, she spent much of her early life in Genoa but returned to Sardinia after the assassination of her brother to become Guidichessa of Arborea and ruled Arborea from 1383 until 1404 when she died of the plague. After her death the resistance gradually yielded and Sardinia fell to the Aragonese. A 19th-century statue of Eleonora, holding a scroll with the *Carta de Logu*, can be seen in the Piazza Eleonora in Oristano.

Fresco in Bosa's church of Nostra Signora di Regnos Altos

shifts of control and influence between Pisa, Genoa and, in the latter part, Aragon, aided and abetted by the Vatican, the Holy Roman Empire and the Sardinians themselves. This instability between the big powers was by and large ended in 1326 when Alfonso IV of Aragon, again with papal backing, effectively took possession of the island after a two-year siege of Cágliari.

The late 14th century saw the rise of Eleonora d'Arborea (*see opposite*), Sardinia's heroine who is often likened to Boudicca or Joan of Arc. Her death marked the climax of a glorious but brief period of Sardinian resistance.

Spanish Rule

Following the marriage of Ferdinand of Aragon and Isabella of Castile in 1479 and hence the unification of the whole of Spain, Sardinia became a province ruled by a Spanish viceroy. The notable events on the island during this period are little

16th-century map of Sardinia

more than symptomatic of the European superpowers' struggle for supremacy in the Mediterranean. In 1541 Charles V, King of Spain and Holy Roman Emperor, visited the island with a vast fleet, en route to flush out a notorious corsair, Hassan Aga who had pillaged Christian ships for his Muslim master. In 1553 Olbia was destroyed by the Turks, who had allied with France against Spain, and half its population was enslaved or deported. Under the feudal system on the island, land was distributed to Spanish nobles who enjoyed absolute power but left the everyday running of their dominions to officials of their own choice. Unsurprisingly, Sardinia became in essence a sleepy, uncared-for backwater of the enormous Spanish Empire. Its rulers cared more for its American colonies (the source of its opulence) and its intractable politico-religious problems than their remoter European possessions.

The War of Spanish Succession, fought between Spain and her rival European powers, largely determined the state of Europe until the Napoleonic Wars. Sardinia, however, was an exception. At the close of the war, through the Treaties of Utrecht and Rastadt (1713 and 1714), the island became part of the Austrian Empire – the Holy Roman part of the erstwhile Spanish Empire – while Sicily passed to the House of Savoy. In 1717 Spain took back Sardinia from the Empire but three years later renounced her claim to the island, which then passed to the House of Savoy. In exchange, Sicily was then ceded to the Austrian Empire by the Savoys.

The Kingdom of Sardinia

The new Kingdom of Sardinia, ruled over in 1720 by Vittorio Amedeo II, comprised the island along with Savoy's enlarged Italian possessions in Savoy, Piedmont and Montferrat. A power of growing significance in Europe, Savoy added further territorial gains during the 18th century. Yet despite policies of investment and limited reform, Sardinia remained feudal and much of its population was opposed to any kind of foreign administration. Centuries of robbery and violence had arisen in the main from hunger and vendetta, the latter being rooted in fierce loyalty to friend and family. It was against this historical background and the slow pace of reform that the Sardinia of the 18th century saw an escalation of banditry; clan warfare, kidnapping and robbery were rife.

During the Napoleonic Wars, Sardinia, uniquely in mainland and Mediterranean Europe, remained unconquered by Bonaparte. In 1793 the French were repulsed from Cágliari by the islanders, and in 1798 Sardinia, along with the kingdom of Sicily, formally entered the war against the French. Nelson's flagship berthed at Sant'Antioco on its way to the Battle of the Nile and his fleet was frequently present around the Straits of Bonifacio in the run-up to the Battle of Trafalgar. The relative security of the island enabled the Savoy royal family to take refuge there during the

Nelson's wish

Nelson coveted the island for the British, writing in despatches: 'If we could possess one island, Sardinia, we should want neither Malta, nor any other'.

Napoleonic Wars. In 1815, as part of the post-Napoleonic settlement, Genoa was added to the kingdom and the kingdom became known as 'Piedmont Sardinia'.

The Savoy rulers were in the main hostile to the escalating liberal movements in Europe and moved only slowly to improve the political and economic conditions of the kingdom. Progress, however, was made under King Carlo Felice (1821–31), who improved the infrastructure and built the Carlo Felice highway running the length of the island (the present-day SS131), and under his successor, Carlo Alberto (1831–49), the feudal system was finally abolished.

19th-century railway remains at Spiaggia Piscinas

Unification

From 1851 to 1861 Sardinia was in the forefront of the Risorgimento (the movement for Italian unification). Carlo Alberto enhanced the cause under Piedmont hegemony by granting a constitution in 1848 and resisting Austrian power in Italy in the first War of Independence (1848–9). His son, Vittorio Emanuele, supported Piedmont's Prime Minister, Count Cavour, in his diplomatic manoeuvres to unite the northern Italian states in the push for unification. But southern Italy, known since 1815 as the Kingdom of the Two Sicilies and with its capital in

Naples, had to be wrested by conquest from its Bourbon masters. Giuseppe Garibaldi led the famous expedition of *I Mille* ('The Thousand'). Starting in 1860, it took him just five months to conquer Sicily and the kingdom of Naples, only halting his march on the papal states to enable Cavour's northern armies to finish the job. On 25 October 1860 Garibaldi handed southern Italy to Cavour. In 1861 Vittorio Emanuele II became king of a united Italy and the Kingdom of Sardinia came to an end.

CAVOUR.
(From a contemporary print in Bianchi's *Cavour*.)

Count Cavour

It could therefore be said that the sleepy island in the Mediterranean, conquered over the centuries by successive waves of military powers, was at the very heart of the Risorgimento. Not only was it the original part of the state at the helm of the politics of unification, but it was also the last home of Giuseppe Garibaldi, the most distinguished soldier of the movement and one of the most skilful guerilla generals in history.

From Unification to the Present

Since Unification Sardinia has had to adapt to the challenge of being part of a major nation state while advancing its own particular interests and retaining its own cultural identity. In the early stages, entrenched colonial attitudes prevailed and much of its resources, such as its forests, were plundered. Mussolini advanced radical social and economic initiatives. Rivers were systematically channelled and dammed, land drainage schemes were carried out and three new towns, Carbonia, Fertilia and Arborea were created. Following World War II the American Rockefeller Foundation piloted a successful scheme to exterminate malaria, which had plagued the island for centuries. Coastal marshes were gradually reclaimed, and could be developed for agriculture and holiday resorts.

World War II saw Cágliari suffer heavy bombing which flattened over half the city. In the wake of the war, movements to advance the independence of the island bore fruit when Sardinia was finally granted a substantial degree of autonomy. Under a special statute of 1948 Sardinia was to be 'an autonomous region with its own legal status'; it now has its own government, the Giunta, appointed by a regional council, elected by proportional representation.

In the 1960s tourism took off with the development of the Costa Smeralda. The glittering coastline continues to entice celebrities (ex premier Berlusconi, Roman Abramovich and Madonna among them), but in 2006 the Sardinian president, Renato Soru, rocked the boat by imposing swingeing taxes on second homes on the coast, large non-Sardinian yachts and private aircraft. Soru has also angered local developers by prohibiting construction of new property in undeveloped areas within 2km (1¼ miles) of the coastline. As a consequence some of the mega-rich summer visitors are now giving Sardinia a wide berth. Meanwhile those without their own planes or yachts are taking advantage of the boom in low-cost carriers to the island.

Messages in murals, Orgósolo

Historical Landmarks

6000–1800BC Neolithic era; tribes settle on the island; first villages built

4000–3000BC (Ozieri culture).

1800–900BC Nuraghic era; large tower-like structures *(nuraghi)* built.

800BC Phoenicians set up trading posts on the island.

7th century BC Greek colonies founded.

6th century BC Carthaginians appropriate coastal regions.

AD227 Sardinia becomes a Roman province.

AD456 Sardinia annexed by the Vandals.

Early 700s Arabs pillage the island, and seize control of part of it in 752.

9th century Contemporary documents record a *'guidice'*, a governing constitutional figure.

1016 Pisa captures Sardinia from the Muslims.

1323–6 The Aragonese take control of Sardinia, with papal backing.

1383–1404 Reign of Eleonora, Regent of Arborea; in 1392 she promulgates the *Carta di Logu* (Code of Laws).

1479 Spain is united on the marriage of Ferdinand of Aragon and Isabella of Castile; Sardinia becomes a province of Spain.

1713–1720 Sardinia ceded to Austria, then to Savoy.

1792–1805 Sardinia remains unconquered during the Napoleonic Wars after declaring war on France in 1798.

1815 Sardinia becomes part of an enlarged Kingdom of Piedmont Sardinia.

1861 Sardinia becomes part of the newly unified Italy.

1943 Cágliari suffers major bomb destruction in World War II.

1947 Malaria is eradicated from the island.

1948 Sardinia is made an autonomous region.

1960s Development of the Costa Smeralda; the island opens up to tourism. Programme of industrialisation.

Mid-1990s Last of the Sardinian mines closed.

2005 Four new Sardinian provinces created: Olbia-Tempio, Ogliastra, Carbonia-Iglesias and Medio-Campidano.

2007 Alghero airport is expanded and improved.

2008 American nuclear submarine base at La Maddalena is shut down.

WHERE TO GO

GETTING AROUND

The island is too large to explore from a single base. If touring, two weeks would be just adequate to sample the different aspects of the coast and the sightseeing highlights, but to see the island comfortably you would need a month. If time is limited to a week or less, make your base in one of the main regions, taking day trips to the coast or forays inland to remote rural areas. The provincial capitals of Cágliari and Sássari are well-worth visiting but are not ideal as tourist bases.

CÁGLIARI AND THE SOUTHEAST

Cágliari

Capital of the island and its main port, **Cágliari** is the most cosmopolitan and modern of Sardinia's cities. Industrial outskirts and traffic-choked streets can be intimidating, but the heart of the old city retains plenty of picturesque charm and historical interest. Along with churches, monuments and museums the city provides the best choice of restaurants and shops on the island and, to the east, a huge sandy beach and flamingo-filled lagoon.

'Karalis' as it was originally named, was one of several settlements in southern Sardinia established as trading posts by the Phoenicians. By the time of Roman rule, it

Tourist trains

The lazy way of seeing the old town of Cágliari is to hop aboard one of the tourist 'trains' which depart from Piazza Carmine in the Stampace quarter. There are seven of these trains a day, except on Mondays during the off-season.

Bastione San Rémy in Cágliari

had become one of the main trading ports of the Mediterranean. The most striking legacy of Roman occupation is the **Anfiteatro** (Amphitheatre; guided visits Tues–Sat 9.30am–1.30pm and 3.30–5.30pm, winter 10am–1pm; admission fee) carved out of the rock on the hillside in the Stampace quarter of the city. The battles between gladiators and beasts drew audiences of 10,000; today the substantial ruins make an evocative setting for concerts, opera and theatre. The town's earliest example of Christian architecture is the heavily restored **Basilica of San Saturnino** on Piazza San Cosimo, in what is now modern Cágliari. Built to commemorate the Sardinian saint who was martyred on this spot in 303, it is a beautiful domed 5th-century cruciform church with a distinctly oriental look.

The bulwarks of Cágliari's medieval defences were built on the hill by the Pisans, who took control in the 13th century. A ring of walls (best seen from afar) was constructed around the city, followed by two defence towers in 1305 and 1307 built in anticipation of Spanish invasions. Pisan concern was not unfounded and the Aragonese put an end to their rule in 1324. Several centuries of Iberian domination finished ingloriously in 1708 when the city yielded to a small Austro-British naval force without so much as a fight.

Castello

On top of the hill, the Pisan- and Aragonese-built **Castello** was the former political, religious and administrative centre. This is the oldest and most interesting quarter of the city, with its monuments, narrow alleys and picturesquely dilapidated dwellings. It is easily covered on foot, though you can hop on one of the tourist 'trains' which depart from Piazza Carmine for a 45-minute guided tour. By foot it's best to start at Piazza Costituzione, then climb the monumental stairway of the **Bastione San Rémy**. The views from the esplanade, where you can sit with a drink, encompass the city, port and lagoons. West of the bastion lies the Pisan-built **Torre dell'Elefante** (Elephant Tower; open summer Tues–Sun 9am–1pm and 3.30–7pm, off-season until 4.30pm; admission fee). The name derives from the little carved elephant which you can see on a plinth on the Via Università side. The tower took on a grisly role under Spanish rule when the severed heads of prisoners were hung in cages above the portcullis. You can admire the views from the tower or those from the terrace of the nearby Caffè Libarium Nostrum (Via Santa Croce) on the city walls.

Cattedrale di Santa Maria

To the east, Piazza Palazzo is flanked by 18th-century buildings and, in one corner, by the striking **Cattedrale di Santa Maria** (Cathedral of Santa Maria; open Mon–Fri 8am–12.30pm and 4–8pm). This Pisan Romanesque church was rebuilt in the 17th century and given a mock Romanesque façade in 1938. The multicoloured interior is essentially baroque but retains marble gems from the original church: the 12th-century pulpits on the entrance wall exquisitely carved with reliefs illustrating *The Life of Christ*, and, in front of the altar, the four lions, each with their prey. The elaborate crypt (entered via a doorway behind the far-right lion) houses the tombs of the Savoy royal family. Next to the cathedral is the much rehashed Archbishop's Palace, and beside it the Palazzo Viceregio, built by the Aragonese for their viceroys. Today it is home to the provincial assembly and occasionally opens to the public for exhibitions.

At the far end of the Piazza, the **Torre di San Pancrazio** (San Pancrazio Tower; open summer Tues–Sun 9am–1pm and 3.30–5.30pm, off-season 9am–4.30pm; admission fee) was built at the highest point of the city to keep guard over vessels sailing through the Gulf of Cágliari. The Aragonese used it as a storehouse and lodging for government officials, and from 1600 it became a prison.

Prize exhibits

The Phoenican, Roman and Byzantine periods are all well represented at the Archaeological Museum, but the prize pieces are the nuraghic *bronzetti*, exquisite and often humorous statuettes of humans and animals which would not look out of place in a stylish modern art gallery.

Citadella dei Musei

At the northern end of Castello, the Citadella dei Musei (Citadel of Museums) is an imaginative cultural centre of gardens and modern museums, incorporating the remains of the Spanish Royal Arsenal. If you choose just one museum make it the **Museo Archeologico Nazionale** (National Museum of Archaeology; open Tues–Sun 9am–8pm; admission fee), housing treasures from major sites throughout the island. Arranged on four floors, the collection provides an overview of successive cultures from Neolithic to early medieval. The upper floors are arranged topographically, focusing on the main nuraghic and Roman sites in the Cágliari province. A cumulative ticket gives you entry to the **Pinacoteca Nazionale** (National Art Gallery; open Tues–Sun 9am–8pm; admission fee) whose most interesting works are the Quattrocento and Cinquecento altarpieces, many of them Catalan.

On an entirely different theme, the nearby **Museo d'Arte Siamese Stefano Cardu** (Cardu Museum of Siamese Art; open mid-June–mid-Sept Tues–Sun 9am–1pm and 4–8pm; off-season 9am–1pm and 3.30–7.30pm; admission fee) is a collection of oriental porcelain, weapons and precious *objets d'art* bequeathed to the city in 1917 by Stefano Cardu. A contractor of public works, credited with the construction of the Royal Palace in Bangkok, Cordu was a Sardinian who lived in Siam (modern-day Thailand) for 20 years, making his fortune and amassing his treasures.

A bizarre collection of anatomical wax models, including macabre cutaway heads and stomachs, is displayed in the **Museo delle Cere Anatomiche di Clemente Susini** (Clemente Susini Museum of Anatomical Waxwork; open Tues–Sun 9am–1pm and 4–7pm; admission fee) near the entrance of the Citadella. This unlikely collection was commissioned in 1801 by Carlo Felice, the Viceroy of Sardinia.

Via Roma

Marina and Stampace

In the lower town, below Castello, Marina is a busy quarter of shops and restaurants. A favourite spot for a stroll or drink is **Via Roma**, whose dignified arcades shelter traditional cafés and elegant boutiques. The street runs parallel to the harbour

Piazza del Carmine Stampace

where huge Terrenia ferries constantly come and go. The network of narrow lanes behind Via Roma teems with trattorias. Via Sardegna has the concentration of eateries, from simple café style to fine dining establishments. This is a pleasant quarter for wandering, with its churches, small food shops and artisans. **Piazza Yenne** to the north is the hub of the Stampace quarter and the starting point of the Carlo Felice highway (SS131), which cuts right through the island to Porto Torres in the north. The road was named after the king who built it, whose statue stands in the square. Stampace is a quarter of historic churches, the most famous of which is **Sant'Efisio** on Via Sant'Efisio. The saint is commemorated every May in one of Sardinia's most spectacular festivals *(see page 95)*.

Poetto

The 6km (4-mile) stretch of sands at Poetto can provide a welcome relief after the sweltering streets of the centre. At the southern end it's not the most peaceful of beaches – facilities include funfairs as well as sun beds and water sports – and the quality of the beach has not been enhanced by the importation of darker sands in 2002. But further north there are still large expanses of unspoilt fine white sands. At night the liveliest spot is Marina Piccola, nestling at the foot of the Sella del Diavolo (Devil's Saddle promontory) at the southern end. Poetto also has the added attraction of a huge colony of flamingoes, along with numerous other waders on the Molentargius marshes behind the beach. The lagoon was formerly used for salt extraction and the name derives from Su Molenti, the donkeys which transported the sacks of salt.

Villasimius

Cágliari's beaches cannot compare with the beautiful stretches of white sand around Villasimius to the east. The resort is reached by a winding road which clings to the mountainous coast, giving glimpses of sandy and pebbly bays below. Off-season, Villasimius is a sleepy village, but throughout the summer visitors flock here for the beaches, gloriously limpid waters and the bustling centre of bars, pizzerias and souvenir shops. Thanks to the short-lived holiday season and the Marine Reserve set up in 1998, which forbids or restricts fishing, deep-sea diving and boating, the

Watersports at Poetto

Maritime Madonna

Just off Isola dei Cavoli, local divers sank a modern statue of the Madonna del Naufrago (Shipwreck Madonna), also known as the Madonna dei Fondali (Our Lady of the Seabed), as a tourist attraction. It lies at a depth of 10m (33ft).

area has retained much of its natural beauty. Some of the best beaches, accessed by dirt tracks, are unsigned; and a visit to the Pro Loco (temporary tourist office) for a map is advisable. The main road south ends near the lighthouse on the **Capo Carbonara**, scene of many a shipwreck over the centuries.

A path leads up to the lighthouse for views of the **Isola dei Cavoli**, an offshore island which can be visited on boat trips from Porto Giunco (a beach not a port) at Villasimius.

Costa Rei

The SS18 follows the coast west and north from Villasimius, affording breathtaking views of the coastline and islets. En route for the Costa Rei you can branch off right to the lovely white sandy beaches of Cala Pira and Cala Sinzias (the latter has a couple of campsites and fills out in high season). Further north is the Costa Rei proper, with its dazzling expanses of white sand and turquoise waters. Developers have taken advantage of this straight stretch of coast, constructing large villa complexes, but happily these don't impose on the beaches themselves. A particularly lovely stretch is the Spiaggia Piscina Rei, with its spacious white sands.

The main centre for the area is **Muravera**, an unremarkable market town surrounded by citrus orchards. If you are returning to Cágliari, there's a beautiful though tortuous route back along the SS125, cutting through the rugged red-walled gorges of the **Monte dei Sette Fratelli** (Mount of the Seven Brothers). The mountains rise to 1,023m (3,355ft) and are one of the rare haunts of the Sardinian stag *(cervo sardo)*.

THE SOUTHWEST

The evocative Punic-Roman ruins of Nora and the extensive Nuraghe Su Nuraxi can be reached easily from Cágliari. Other highlights of the southwest are the abandoned mines of Iglesiente, the glorious beaches of the Costa Verde and the islands of San Pietro and Sant'Antióco.

Pula and Nora

An uninspiring route via refineries and salt works takes you south from Cágliari to the town of Pula. Despite the industry, many species of wading birds inhabit the Stagno di Santa Gilla marshes. To the south the main centre is **Pula**, a busy little town with a useful tourist office and the small Museo Archeologico Patroni (open daily 9am–one hour before sunset; admission fee) with finds from the nearby archaeological

Remains of the Punic Temple of Tanit at Nora

site of **Nora** (same hours as museum; cumulative ticket available). Founded by the Phoenicians, then built over by Carthaginians and Romans, the city is peacefully set on the Capo di Pula promontory, overlooked by a 16th-century Spanish watchtower. Excavations have revealed extensive relics including the Punic Temple of Tanit (goddess of fertility), Roman baths with mosaics and an impressive Roman theatre where performances are staged in mid-summer. Overlooking the nearby beach, the chapel of Sant'Efisio is the pilgrimage church of Cágliari's famous Festival of Sant'Efisio in early May *(see page 95)*. **Santa Margherita**, southwest of Pula, was developed in the 1960s as an upmarket resort. Luxury hotels are discreetly hidden among gardens and pines, with direct access to the ribbon of white sands. But for the best beaches and a more beautiful coastline head south to **Chia** and beyond. The Saracen watchtower on a hillock here commands a great vista of the dazzling white sands and dunes stretching towards Capo Spartivento.

Costa del Sud

The corniche road which snakes its way from Capo Spartivento to Porto di Teulada affords a magnificent panorama of sheer cliffs, rugged promontories and deep turquoise waters. Cala Tuerredda, one of the few beaches along the predominantly rocky coast, is a sublime spot for a cooling dip. The coast road comes to an end at Porto di Teulada; the promontory to the west is a military zone and the beaches at Capo Teulada are accessible only by boat trips in July and August, departing from Porto di Teulada.

Isola di Sant'Antióco

Off the southwest coast, the island of Sant'Antióco has been connected to the mainland by a causeway since Carthaginian times. The Romans built a bridge across the Golfo di Palmas,

Burial urns at Sant'Antióco

remains of which you can still see at the far end of the causeway. Ignore the industrial port and head for the historic upper
town signed from the seafront. This ancient town, believed
to be the first Phoenician colony in Sardinia, became a thriving port and traded in the locally mined lead, zinc and gold.
Originally called Sulcis, a name subsequently given to
the whole region, its present-day name commemorates Saint
Antiochus, an African slave who was tortured by the Romans,
tossed into the sea and washed up on the shores of the island.
After converting the locals to Christianity, he was martyred
in AD127 and is buried in the early Christian catacombs of the
Chiesa di Sant'Antióco (Church of Sant'Antióco; guided
tours of catacombs Mon–Sat 9am–noon and 3–6pm, Sun
10–11am and 3–6pm; admission fee). These fascinating catacombs were created from former Punic tombs and comprise
dark, low-lying chambers with niches, some retaining their
skeletons or fragments of frescoes.

Sea silk

In Sant'Antióco's Museum of Ethnography look out for samples of the *pinna nobilis*, the huge mollusc from the lagoons which produce byssus – the tufts of silky filaments by which the molluscs adhere to the rock. Known as *seta del mare* (sea silk) the thread was used to make ties, gloves, shawls and other garments until the 1930s.

From Piazza de Gaspari, take Via Castello up to the archaeological site, passing en route the Piedmontese Su Pisu fort (open daily 9am– 1pm and 3.30–7pm; admission fee), the remains of the Punic necropolis (on the right) and the acropolis (on the left). The **tophet** (same hours as fort; admission fee) is a sacred site for the ashes of babies and infants *(see Tharros, page 47)*. Clusters of orange funerary urns lie among the rocks – these are mainly reproduction. The new **Museo Archeologico** (same hours as tophet; cumulative ticket available) houses finds from the ancient city of Sant'Antióco and the Sulcis region as a whole. Retracing your footsteps, it's worth making a small detour to the **Museo Etnografico** (Ethnographical Museum; same opening times as Museo Archeologico) at Via Necrópoli which focuses on farming, bread- and cheese-making, and other local traditions.

The subterranean chambers of the Punic or Carthaginian Necropolis beyond the museum can be visited with a (non-English-speaking) guide. These small interconnecting chambers were inhabited for centuries, the last inhabitants being ejected in the 1960s for reasons of hygiene.

Culture apart, Sant'Antióco is a hilly island, with rocky outcrops and cliffs on the west coast, and accessible beaches on the eastern and southern coasts. **Calasetta**, 10km (6 miles) northwest of Sant'Antióco, has a couple of nearby beaches and a port with a regular ferry service to Carloforte on the island of San Pietro.

Isola di San Pietro

Legend has it that St Peter took refuge on this small, rocky island following a shipwreck, hence the name San Pietro. The first inhabitants were a colony of Ligurians who emigrated here from the Tunisian island of Tabarqa. Descendants of fishermen and coral-gatherers who had settled on the African island in the 16th century, they were bequeathed the island of San Pietro in 1738 by King Carlo Emanuele III of Savoy, who was seeking to repopulate Sardinia. Having been subjected to Saracen raids on Tabarqa, the Ligurians then became victims of a French invasion of San Pietro in 1792 and five years later to Saracen slave raids.

Over two centuries later, the inhabitants of the island still speak a Genoese dialect and the local cuisine (which is some of the best in Sardinia) features Ligurian and North African specialities, as well as more general Mediterranean ones.

From the Sardinian mainland, San Pietro is easily reached by a 35-minute car ferry from the small harbour of Portovesme on the southwest coast. Leaving behind the view of belching chimneys of nearby Portoscuro, the ferries ply across to San Pietro's delightful port of **Carloforte**. The waterfront area, overlooked by pastel-washed houses, bustles with

Carloforte

The mattanza

In early summer, shoals of tuna swim through the waters between San Pietro, Sant'Antióco and Portoscuso en route to the Black Sea. Fishermen use a system of nets to channel the tuna into the *camera della morte*, or death-chamber. Once the chamber is full, the fish are hauled out of the water and bludgeoned to death. Though definitely not a pretty sight, the *mattanza*, or tuna massacre, inevitably attracts crowds.

fishing boats, ferries and pleasure craft. The town has a handful of small hotels, a string of seaview restaurants and cafés, and pleasant walks along the waterfront. The hub is Piazza Carlo Emanuele III, dominated by a large statue of the king. The small and attractively laid out **Museo Civico**, housed in the Carlo Emanuele III fort, has sections on tuna fishing (including gruesome-looking gaffs and axes used for the *mattanza*), transportation of minerals and island history.

San Pietro's coast is best seen by boat. A typical half-day tour of the island takes in grottoes, cliff scenery and otherwise inaccessible beaches. There is no coastal road that does the full circuit of the island, though you can gain access to the main beaches, as well as Capo Sándalo in the west with its towering cliffs and rare falcons and the Punta delle Colonne in the south, named after the rock stacks that rise sheer from the crystalline waters.

Iglésias

For the capital of a mining region, **Iglésias** is a surprisingly appealing town. It lies in the centre of the Iglesiente, the mountainous region west of Cágliari renowned for rich mineral deposits. Silver and lead were exploited by Phoenicians, Carthaginians and Romans, after which the mines were abandoned until the 13th century when Ugolino della Cherardesca, the tyrannical Pisan leader who featured in Dante's

Inferno, founded Iglésias and rekindled the industry. From the mid-19th century the mining activities focused on zinc.

The hub of the town is **Piazza Sella**, a large square where locals relax on tree-shaded benches and boys race on cycles around the statue of Quintino Sella (the minister responsible for re-opening the mines). The castle tower off the square is one of the few vestiges of the Pisan-built medieval fortifi-

Piazza Sella in Iglésias

cations. From the Piazza, Corso Matteoti, lined by elegant boutiques, brings you into the Aragonese-built old town. With its medieval (and later) churches, pedestrianised streets and Spanish-style houses with beautiful balconies, this quarter makes for a delightful stroll. The central Piazza Municipio is overlooked by the **Cattedrale di Santa Chiara** (Santa Chiara Cathedral), its simple but striking Romanesque/Gothic façade belying a rich 17th-century interior (currently closed for restoration). The cathedral faces the neoclassical **Municipio** (Town Hall), while the south side of the square is filled with the Bishop's Palace.

Tempio di Antas

North of Iglésias, the SS126 winds through the mountains towards the ruins of the Roman **Tempio di Antas** (Temple of Antas; open May–Sept daily 9.30am–one hour before sunset, off-season Sat–Sun 9.30am–4pm; admission fee). The origins are believed to be nuraghic, though the present-day

Buggeru with its abandoned mine buildings

ruins are those of a Roman temple built over a 3rd-century BC Carthaginian sanctuary. The site was discovered in the 1960s and the remaining columns were re-erected in the portico of the temple chamber. This is a delightfully remote spot with walks along *macchia*-scented footpaths. The nearby **Grotta Su Mannau** (guided tours Easter–Oct 9.30am–6.30pm; admission fee), signposted off the SS126, is a series of caves with some spectacular stalagmites and stalactites.

Mining Centres

The once-flourishing mining industry has left its mark on the region with abandoned mine shafts and industrial plants scarring the rugged landscapes and cliffs. The main mines have been opened as tourist attractions, but apart from July and August, guided tours are by appointment only. Closest to Iglésias is the lead and zinc **Monteponi** mine, southwest of town (tel: 0781 491300; guided tours of its Galleria Villamarina weekdays 8.30am–5pm, weekends 8.30am–1pm; reservations required; admission fee).

On the coast, the main Iglésias beach of Fontanamare is a huge, sweeping stretch of unspoilt sands. The road north follows the contours of the coast, providing a visual feast of sheer cliffs, rocky outcrops and views of the strangely shaped **Scoglio Pan di Zuchero** (Sugarloaf Rock) jutting out of the sea. Abandoned mines can be seen at Nebida and at Porto Flavia at Masua where ore was loaded onto cargo ships. **Buggeru** was one of the main mining centres, founded in the mid-18th century. Formerly it was only accessible by boat; now it's a seaside resort, with sandy beaches, a port for pleasure craft and the prominent remains of the mines. (For guided tours of the Galleria Henry tel: 0781 491300.) The loveliest beaches in the region are **Cala Domestica** to the south, set at the end of an inlet and **Spiaggia Portixeddu** to the north, a huge expanse of sands, backed by towering dunes.

Costa Verde

The coast north of Capo Pécora remains remarkably unspoilt by tourism. The name (Green Coast) alludes to the *macchia* which carpets the dunes and rocks. The beaches here are stunning, but the best have to be accessed by twisting mountain roads and/or dirt tracks. The legendary **Piscinas** beach has 9km (5 miles) of sands, with huge dunes rising up to 50m (160ft). The only development along this remote, desert-like landscape is the chic **Hotel Le Dune**, converted from an old mine building. A dirt track north of Spiaggia Piscinas follows the coast to the small beach resorts of **Porto Maga** and **Marina di Arbus**. The last resort before Oristano province is **Torre dei Corsari**, an untidy sort of place, but graced by a beautiful beach backed by dunes. Inland from Piscinas the mine shafts and buildings in and around the hill town of **Montevecchio** are a legacy of its once-thriving industry. Guided tours (tel: 0781 491300; five times daily in summer) take in the miners' houses, hospital and church, and an exhibition on the life of the mining community.

Crowning a nearby hill at Villanovaforru is the **Nuraghe di Genna Maria** (open daily 9.30am–1pm and 3.30–5.30pm or 7pm, depending on season; admission fee), whose main attraction is the 360-degree panorama which, weather permitting, encompasses almost half the island. But if your interest is purely archaeological, skip this one and head for Sardinia's oldest and most extensive *nuraghe* ruins: **Su Nuraxi** at Barumini (open daily in summer 9am–7pm, off-season until dusk; admission fee). Guided tours (normally in Italian only, possible queues in summer) are compulsory, though you can get quite a good view of the central section from the roadside. The imposing central tower is only two-thirds of its original height with only two of the three storeys still intact. Built around 1500BC, it was later fortified by ramparts and corner towers which still stand. A village developed around the fortifications with about 200 circular dwellings, some of which have been reconstructed. The decline came with the Carthaginian invasion of the 6th century BC, though the site was partially reconstructed and inhabited until Roman times. The complex as a whole is best seen from the top of the central tower – from here, too, you have good views of a ruined 12th-century castle crowning a remarkably conical hill to the south.

Wild Horses of Giara di Gésturi

This extensive plateau north of Barumini is home to abundant wildlife, and in particular famous for *cavallini* – the small wild horses, distinguished by their dark manes and almond-shaped eyes. The species has been protected since the 1960s and the number roaming on the plain has risen to around 600. You are most likely to see them at the ponds known as *paulis* – apart from the summer months when the water evaporates. To reach the plateau follow the Altopiano signs from Gésturi. A Didactic Centre provides information on the plateau and printed details (in English) on the various footpaths, both botanical and archaeological.

The rocky west coast

ORISTANO AND THE WEST

The least known of Sardinia's provinces, Oristano has no international airport (the nearest are Cágliari and Alghero) and the region is largely ignored by tourists. The coast is one of cliffs, rocky promontories and long, deserted stretches of beach. Major cultural highlights are the ancient city of Tharros and the Sinis Peninsula, the well-preserved nuraghic complexes of Losa and Santa Catarina and the centre of the provincial capital, Oristano.

Oristano

When the once-flourishing port of Tharros was finally defeated by Saracen raids in the 11th century, the inhabitants moved inland and resettled at the small village of Oristano. It became the capital of the Guidicato of Arborea (one of Sardinia's four autonomous territories) and in the 14th century

Masked equestrian at the Sa Sartiglia festival in Oristano

flourished under the rule of the warrior, Eleonora of Arborea *(see page 16)*. Following her death in 1404 the region fell into decline and today only vestiges survive of the medieval fortifications.

Oristano is the capital of the province and the only main town of western Sardinia. The dignified town centre is well worth a visit, particularly the 19th-century **Piazza Eleonora**, presided over by a large statue of the town's heroine, the elegant **Corso Umberto** and the town's main musem. The city walls were demolished long ago and the only remaining medieval fortifications are the **Torre di San Mariano II** (also called Torre di San Cristóforo) in Piazza Roma and the nearby Portixedda (Little Tower). The other main landmark of the centre is the beautiful onion-domed octagonal bell tower of the **Cattedrale di Santa Maria** (Cathedral of Santa Maria; open Mon–Sat 7am–noon and 4–7pm, Sun 8am–1pm) on Piazza Mannu. The church was built in 1228 but underwent a major baroque revamp in the 17th century. If your next stop after Oristano is the ancient city of Tharros, don't miss the **Antiquarium Arborense** (open daily 9am–2pm and 3–8pm, later on some summer weekdays; admission fee) in the Palazzo Parpaglia on Piazza Corrias. This excellent archaeological museum displays a collection of finds from Tharros and the Sinis Peninsula: nuraghic ceramics and tools, Phoenician jugs, weapons and jewellery, Punic pottery and Roman amphorae, glassware and gemstones. The small art gallery focuses on 15th- and 16th-century altarpieces, which show a marked Catalan influence.

On a hillock 3km (2 miles) south of the city, the **Basilica of Santa Giusta** is a beautiful example of the Pisan Romanesque style. A former cathedral which would have enjoyed uninterrupted views of the lagoon prior to Santa Giusta's modern development, it is a lofty three-naved church with granite and marble columns plundered from Tharros and the nearby Roman city of Neapolis. The frescoed Renaissance chapels were added in the 16th century, and the campanile in 1875 to replace the old one that collapsed.

Sa Sartiglia

Oristano is at its liveliest between the last Sunday of Carnival and Shrove Tuesday when it hosts the famous Sa Sartiglia festival. This flamboyant three-day affair is rooted in pagan rituals guaranteeing the return of spring. Weeks ahead of the festival two kings (or Componidori) are chosen for their equestrian expertise; one is the king of the Guild of Farmers, the other of the Guild of Carpenters. The main event is the Corso dell'Anello joust when the horsemen, and especially the Componidori, clad in masks and medieval costume, charge down a long, wide track lunging their spears at a small star-shaped ring suspended on a rope. The more rings that are lanced, especially by the Componidori, the better the chance for the oncoming harvest. In the final ride, the Componidori lies down face-up on his horse, blessing the audience with periwinkles and violets. The Corso dell'Anello is followed by La Pariglia, with participants performing extraordinary equestrian feats. On the following day children take part in a mini Sa Sartiglia, riding *cavallini*, the little horses from the Giara di Gésturi (see page 42).

Quartz sand at Is Arútas on the Sinis Peninsula

The Sinis Peninsula

Northwest of Oristano the Sinis is a low-lying peninsula of white sand beaches, marshes and flamingo-filled lagoons. **Cabras** is the main town, set on a large lagoon (the Stagno di Cabras) which is the source of the mullet offered in various forms in the many local fish restaurants. The Museo Cívico on the banks of the lagoon (open Apr–Sept 9am–1pm and 4–8pm, winter 3–7pm; admission fee) displays treasures salvaged from Tharros, and the prehistoric site at Cuccuru is Arrius, 3km (2 miles) southwest of Cabras. The ethnographical section features samples of the traditional *fassonis*, flat-bottomed fishing boats made of rushes and formerly used on the lagoons.

The deserted village of **San Salvatore**, west of Cabras, featured in several spaghetti Westerns in the 1960s. The only event that wakes the village these days is the Festival of San Salvatore in late August and early September. Pilgrims who come to celebrate the nine-day event stay in the huddle of little houses or *cumbessias*. The fascinating Church of San Salvatore (open in season Mon–Sat 9.30am–1pm and 3.30–6pm) originated around a nuraghic sanctuary, which was constructed over a sacred well. Inside, steps lead down to the subterranean chambers where you can see an altar dedicated to Mars and Venus and fragments of wall frescoes, drawings and graffiti dating back to Punic, Roman, Arab and Spanish times.

Just before Tharros, the **Church of San Giovanni di Sinis** is, with San Saturnino in Cágliari *(see page 26)*, the oldest Christian monument in Sardinia. It was originally built in the 5th century and, though much restored, retains its Greek cross form and Byzantine style. The church fell into ruins in the 1820s and was used as a shelter for shepherds and animals.

The ancient city of **Tharros** was founded by the Phoenicians around 730BC at the southern tip of the Sinis Peninsula. Under the Carthaginians it became one of the most important trading ports of the western Mediterranean. The Romans improved the city with streets, baths and an aqueduct; but from the 7th century Saracen raids marked the fate of the city and by 1070 it had fallen into decline. Two-thirds of the site is submerged underwater, due to subsidence, but excavations have revealed substantial Roman and, to a lesser extent, Punic remains. Dominating the ruins on the eastern slope, and rising theatrically above the sea are two white columns from a Roman temple. Other relics, including a cistern, forum, thermal baths and small temple are not as easily identifiable, though the pamphlet from the information office will help to identify the main landmarks. To the north the Carthaginians built a tophet *(see box below)* and an acropolis on the hill, over the remains of a large nuraghic settlement.

Punic Tophets

Although ancient Greek historians described tophets as Punic sites where infants were cruelly sacrificed to the gods, modern-day archaeologists believe they were sanctuaries for the ashes of stillborn babies or deceased infants. Cremation rituals often entailed the sacrifice of small animals; the ashes were then placed in an urn beside a sacred stone decorated with symbolic figures of gods. These Punic sites date from the 5th to the 3rd century BC.

If you're looking to cool off after exploring the ruins, the nearby beach of San Giovanni di Sinis is more sheltered than those north of Tharros and less crowded than Oristano's main beach, Marina di Torre Grande. The beaches to the north, often pounded by huge rollers, afford some spectacular scenery. **Is Arútas** is one of the loveliest, composed of grains of shiny white quartz and washed by crystal-clear waters. Further north the resort of Putzu Idu is a departure point for boat trips to the **Isola di Mal di Ventre**, 10km (6 miles) offshore. Commonly mistranslated as Stomach Ache Island, the name actually derives from *Malu Entu* or evil wind, after the strong mistral which blows for most of the year. The longest and most exposed of the beaches is **Is Arenas** which boasts 6km (4 miles) of undeveloped sands backed by dense woods of pine and acacia. To the north the picturesque beach resort of **S'Archittu** is named after a natural limestone arch where locals leap into the beautiful clear waters of the inlet.

A dirt track off the main road leads to the ruins of **Cornus**, site of the last revolt of the Carthaginian and Sardinian forces against Roman rule in 216BC. Saracen raids in the 10th century forced the inhabitants to desert the town and set up inland – at present day **Cuglieri**. On the western slopes of Monte Ferru, the village can be spotted from afar by the silver dome of the Basilica di Santa Maria della Neve.

The Interior

The dominant feature of northern Oristano is **Monte Ferru** (Iron Mountain), an ancient volcanic mass formed of trachyte and basalt. Forests of oak and sweet chestnut flourish on the mountain slopes; lower down, particularly around Seneghe, the olive groves are said to produce some of the best olive oil in Italy. The main village is **Santa Lussurgiu**, set inside the crater on the eastern slopes. The traditional pursuits of the region, including leatherwork, carpentry, weaving and winemaking are displayed in the Museo della Tecnologia Contadina (tel: 0783 550617; by appointment only; admission fee) on Via Deodato Meloni. From the village a scenic mountain road takes you to San Leonardo di Siete Fuentes, renowned for its mineral waters.

Santa Cristina and Nuraghe Losa

Northeast of Oristano, and easily accessible from the SS131 highway to Sássari, are two of Sardinia's major archaeological sites. **Santa Cristina** (open daily 8.30am–11pm, off-season 8.30am–9pm; admission fee), lying among olive groves, was a major nuraghic settlement. Excavations revealed extensive remains including dwellings, a 15m (50ft) high tower and, most significant of all, a well-temple in a remarkably good state of preservation, dating possibly from the 1st millennium BC. The **Church of Santa Cristina** was built on the site in c1200, and the huts you see around it, known as *muristenes*, are used by pilgrims who come to worship during the Santa Cristina festival days – the only time the church is open. Finds from the well-temple can be seen in the Museo Archeologico-Etnografico (Archaeological-Ethnographical Museum) in the Palazzo Atzori in **Pauli-látino**, 5km (3 miles) northeast of Santa Cristina.

Olive groves at Santa Cristina

Continue heading along the SS131 for the **Nuraghe Losa** (open daily 9am–one hour before sunset; admission fee; <www.nuraghelosa.net>). The focal point here is a massive keep dating back to 1500BC. This is surrounded by ramparts, minor towers and outer walls, all of which were added at a later date. You can gain access to the *nuraghe* through a narrow passageway to see the vaulted chambers and, from the terrace (depending on the weather) the peaks of the Gennargentu mountains.

East of Nuraghe Losa, Ghilarza's main claim to fame is as the birthplace of Antonio Gramsci, one of the founders of the Italian Communist Party in 1921. The town is now home to the Casa di Gramsci research and study centre. Gramsci links apart, Ghilarza is an uninspiring sort of place.

South of Ghilarza, **Fordongianus** – or Forum Traiani as it was originally called – was founded by the Romans after the discovery of hot springs. Impressive remains of the baths or **Terme Romane** (open daily summer 9am–1pm and 3–8pm, off-season 2.30–5pm; admission charge) can be seen on the banks of the River Tirso, where the main stream gushes out at a temperature of 54°C (130°F). The steaming waters here are still occasionally used to wash clothes by local women (who claim the results are superior to those of modern washing machines). Fordongianus is distinctive for the red trachyte stone used in the churches, houses and the modern outdoor sculpture for which it is renowned. The most notable house is the late 16th-century **Casa Aragonese** in the centre, a restored Catalan noble's dwelling which preserves its porticoed entrance and decorated Gothic-Aragonese doorways and windows.

South of Oristano, **Arborea** was founded in 1928 as the main focus of Benito Mussolini's agricultural development scheme. The River Tirso was dammed, a huge expanse of marshland drained and scores of new farms established for settlers from northern Italy. It is still a rich and fertile region.

NUORO AND THE EAST

The province of Nuoro covers the mountainous heart of Sardinia, a region of wild landscapes and remote villages and towns. Notorious for banditry, Nuoro has not traditionally endeared itself to travellers. Today, however, the interior is opening up to trekkers, climbers, spelaeologists – or those just curious to see Sardinia at its most Sard. The region stretches to the eastern coastline, fringed by enticing bays and pristine waters.

Sardinia's mountainous heart

Nuoro

Its location, on a great granite plateau facing the rocky heights of the Sopramonte, is the most striking aspect of the province's capital. The town itself has limited tourist appeal, lacking picturesque charm and surrounded by modern sprawl; but it's pleasantly uncommercialised and has some interesting literary links and an excellent ethnographical museum. The **Corso Garibaldi**, the main shopping street, cuts through the old town and leads into the central Piazza San Giovanni. Off the Corso on Via Sebastiano Satta, the **Museo d'Arte Nuoro** or MAN (Museum of Nuorese Art; open Tues–Sun 10am–1pm and 4.30–8.30pm; admission fee) makes a stylish setting for temporary exhibitions and a permanent collection of works of art by leading 19th- to 21st-century Sardinian artists. In Via

Mannu the **Museo Archeo-logico Nazionale** (National Museum of Archaeology; open Tues–Sat 9am–1.30pm, Wed–Thur also 3–5pm) has a small but impressive collection of local archaeological finds, ranging from neolithic to medieval. More popular, however, is the **Museo della Vita e delle Tradizioni Popolari Sarde** (Museum of Sardinian Life and Popular Traditions; open mid-June–Sept daily 9am–8pm; Oct–mid-June daily 9am–1pm and 3–7pm; admission fee),

Mask on display in Nuoro's Museum of Sardinian Life

on the southern edge of town at Via Antonio Mereu 56. The collection gives an excellent insight into local traditions, crafts and festivals. Exhibits include some exquisite costumes and textiles, musical instruments and, most striking of all, sinister figures with black wooden masks, sheepskin clothing and strings of cow bells dangling on their backs. During local carnivals similarly clad figures perform ritual dances, culminating in a symbolic 'killing' of the scapegoat.

Nuoro is renowned as the birthplace of leading Sardinian *literati*, among them the prolific Grazia Deledda (1871–1936), winner of the Nobel Prize for Literature in 1926. Although she married young and moved to Russia, her 50 or so novels are set in her native Nuoro and portray the passions of its people. The author's house in Via Grazia Deledda, tucked away in the atmospheric Santu Predu quarter, is now the **Museo Deleddiano** (Deleddiano Museum; open mid-June–Sept Tues–Sat 9am–8pm; Oct–mid-June 9am–1pm and 3–

7pm; admission fee) devoted to Deleddiano memorabilia (in Italian only). Nuoro was also home to Sardinia's most famous poet, Sebastiano Satta. Small bronze statues of the poet can be seen in **Piazza Sebastiano Satta** where he lived.

From Nuoro you can see the village of **Oliena** across the valley, dominated by the slopes of Monte Corrasi. The setting is dramatic but there is not a lot to detain you in the grey stone centre. The town is mainly used as a launching pad for hiking and climbing in the Sopramonte di Oliena. The old quarter is the most compelling part of town and, with its impossibly narrow sloping streets, is best seen on foot. The Oliena region is known for its excellent Cannonau wine.

Orgósolo

South of Oliena, **Orgósolo**, the 'bandit capital of Sardinia', lies deep in the wild Sopramonte mountains. The setting is dramatic and there is a certain fascination about its notorious past, but Orgósolo itself is an unpicturesque town, fringed by dreary apartment blocks. Signs are peppered with bullet holes and the many **murals**, immortalising the vendettas, add to the slightly sinister feel of the place. The first murals appeared in the 1960s and were followed by scenes depicting political or

Banditry in the Barbagia

The scene of kidnapping and violence in the 1950s and 60s, Orgósolo earned itself the reputation as the capital of banditry. The violence, rooted in feuds between local shepherds and farmers, was immortalised in Vittorio De Seta's award-winning film, *Banditi a Orgósolo* (Bandits at Orgósolo) in 1961. From 1960–9 there were 414 murders and countless kidnappings on the island, mainly by shepherds in the Barbagia region. But Orgósolo had long been a centre of vendettas. From 1901–54 there was on average a murder in the village every two months.

social themes. Today there are more than 150, many of them vibrant and accomplished works of art. The most recent additions depict 9/11 and the toppling of Saddam Hussein.

If you happen to be in the region in mid-January or at carnival time in February head straight for **Mamoiada** west of Orgosolo. The town is famous for its masked festivities *(see page 94)* and has a **Museo delle Maschere** (Mask Museum; open Tues–Sun 9am–1pm and 3–7pm; admission fee) in Piazza Europa. Handcrafted masks are also sold locally.

The Gennargentu National Park

The Barbagia centres on the Gennargentu, a great granite massif whose name, Silver Gate, derives from the shimmering effect of the sun on the snowy slopes. This wild and remote region covers 59,000 hectares (146,000 acres), and, at **Punta La Marmora** rises to 1,834m (6,015ft), the highest peak in Sardinia. From here views encompass almost the entire island. The granite mountain peaks are barren but the lower slopes are carpeted in forests of oak and chestnut. In winter skiers take to the slopes of Bruncu Spina near **Fonni**, which at 1,000m (3,280ft) is the highest town in Sardinia. Further south, the village of **Aritzo**, amid forests of sweet chestnut, is pleasantly refreshing in summer and enjoys fine views of the mountains. In former times the village sold chests of snow throughout the island, and you can see the straw-lined boxes used to transport it in the **Museo Etnografico** (Ethnographical Musem; open Tues–Sun 10am–1pm and 4–7pm, winter until 6pm; admission fee).

East Coast

Gloriously unspoilt beaches are the main draw of Nuoro's east coast. In the north, along the Costa degli Oleandi (Oleander Coast), **Posada** is a gem of a village, huddled below the tower of its ruined medieval **Castello della Fava** (Bean

Posada and the Castello della Fava

Castle; open daily 9am–1pm and 3–6pm; admission fee). Posada flourished as a military stronghold in medieval times, but pirate attacks and malaria took their toll. The hilltop tower and ruined walls command sweeping views of the sea, river and surrounding fertile plain. The village lies inland from a huge stretch of undeveloped but exposed sandy beach.

Orosei

Orosei is the capital of the Baronia region, dominated on the western side by the long barren ridge of Monte Albo. Land here was reclaimed after the eradication of malaria and today the fertile plains are planted with citrus orchards, olive groves and vineyards. A flourishing coastal port in late medieval times, the town was forced inland by the silting up of the River Cedrino. It is one of Nuoro's more appealing towns, with a lively central square, some fine churches and excellent beaches nearby. The town's heart is the **Piazza del Pópolo**,

Bidderosa beach

The Orosei coast is fringed by beaches, marshes and pines. The loveliest beach here is Bidderosa, edging the protected Bidderosa Park. The number of visitors and cars is restricted and in high season you are asked to obtain a pass from the forest station of Bidderosa on the SS125 at the park entrance (tel: 0784 998367).

overlooked by the **Catte-drale di San Giácomo**. The showpiece of Orosei, the cathedral has a fine tower and five tiled cupolas, though is rather spoilt by the neo-classical façade added at a later date. Nearby, Piazza Sas Ánimas is flanked by the Chiesa delle Ánime and the remains of the grim-looking castle which became the Pri-gione Vecchia (Old Prison).

The town's oldest church, though much restored, is the 15th-century Chiesa di Sant'Antonio on the eponymous piazza.

Dorgali and the Golfo di Orosei

The road south from Orosei twists down to **Dorgali**, a town on the southern fringes of the Baronia, overlooking valleys of vineyards and olive trees. About 8km (5 miles) before the town a road branches off to the **Grotta di Ispinigoli** (Ispinigoli Cave; open daily for tours on the hour from 9am–1pm and 3–6pm, off-season until 5pm; admission fee). This huge chamber was discovered in the 1950s by shepherds shel-tering from a storm. The findings of Phoenician jewellery and the bones of a 10-year- old-girl suggest the cave was used for human sacrifice. *Ispinigoli* or 'thorn of the grotto' refers to the 38m (125ft) stalagmite which claims to be the largest in Europe and the second largest in the world. This striking column links the floor to the vault – the top metre is in fact a stalactite, while 37m (121ft) have grown from the ground, a process which has taken around four million years.

Dorgali is a major centre of handicrafts, particularly leather, hand-woven carpets, embroidered shawls, ceramics and gold filigree. Occasionally you can see craftsmen at work, throwing a pot or creating haversack-like leather 'shepherd's bags'. The region is liberally endowed with archaeological sites, caves and canyons; the tourist office on Piazza Italia can supply you with details of the many guided trips – you can choose between jeep, foot, kayak, bus, bike or horse.

Three kilometres (2 miles) south of Dorgali, the road to the coast corkscrews through terraced vineyards and oak trees, then plunges under the limestone rock before emerging at the glistening sea of **Cala Gonone**. Tucked below the mountains, this is the only real resort for the **Golfo di Orosei** to the south, a ravishing coastline of limestone cliffs and pristine beaches, lapped by waters of every imaginable shade of blue and green. This 20km (12-mile) stretch is inaccessible by car, and the port of Cala Gonone does a roaring summer trade in boat excursions. Choose between the sea shuttle, sailing boats or motor cruises. Alternatively you can hire your own motorised dinghy (no experience required). The cliffs are riddled with deep grottoes, the most renowned of which is the **Grotta del Bue Marino** (Grotto of the Sea Ox; guided tours; admission fee). This spectacular cave, full of weird and wonderful shapes, is named after the rare monk seal which used to breed here. After the

The Golfo di Orosei

cave was opened to the public (in the 1940s) the seals gradually began to disappear. The next beach down is **Cala Luna**, a sublime spot (until the boatloads arrive) with towering cliffs, caves, *macchia*-covered rocks and oleanders. Another beauty spot is Cala Sisine, the next beach on; but the real gems are further south at **Cala Mariolu** and **Cala di Goloritzè**.

On a volcanic plain 11km (7 miles) northwest of Dorgali, **Serra Orrios** (open for guided tours only; Apr–June and Sept 9am–noon and 3–5pm; July–Aug 9am–noon and 4–6pm; winter 9am–noon and 2–4pm; admission fee) was one of the largest nuraghic settlements on the island. It spreads over 6,000 sq m (7,200 sq yds) and may have accommodated 600–700 villagers. Seventy huts have been discovered, along with two temples, but that's only half of it – it is thought another 120–130 huts are still to be exhumed.

West of Dorgali, **Su Gologone** has two claims to fame: the Sorgente Su Gologone, which is the largest spring in Sardinia, and the charming Su Gologone Hotel with a restaurant renowned throughout the island for delicious Barbagia cuisine *(see page 132)*. Su Gologone is also the starting point for the highly recommended hike to Valle Lanaittu and **Monte Tìscali**. In the late 19th century woodcutters discovered the remains of a nuraghic village, concealed at the foot of a huge cave within the mountain itself. The dwellings were squat and tower-like with walls of limestone blocks and roofs of juniper wood. Today only traces remain, but excavations continue. From the Valle di Lanaitto where you must leave the car, it's a 1½–2-hour relatively strenuous hike up the mountain. Provided you're reasonably fit it's worth going for the walk alone. The path is waymarked by red triangles for most of the route, but a guide is recommended (ask at the tourist office in Oliena or Dorgali). South of Tiscali the Su Gorroppu canyon *(see page 91)* offers some spectacular hiking, preferably with a guide.

The inviting Costa Smeralda

COSTA SMERALDA AND THE NORTHEAST

The city of Olbia is the gateway to the Costa Smeralda, a small stretch of wild coastline which was transformed into an exclusive holiday area for the rich and famous. Beyond it lies Palau, launching pad for the lovely islands of the Maddalena Archipelago, and further north the popular resort of Santa Teresa Gallura, surrounded by enticing beaches. The granite coastline, with its wind-carved rocks, is a dramatic feature of this northeastern corner of the island.

Olbia

The development of the Costa Smeralda led to the creation of an international airport at Olbia and an unprecedented boost to the city's economy. Since tourism took off here, the population has trebled (it is now the third largest town in Sardinia), and the ferry port, being closest to the mainland, is the busiest on the island. Visitors arriving at its airport justifiably ignore the town centre and head straight for the resorts. It is one of the oldest cities in Sardinia, but only traces survive from its Punic, Roman and medieval past. The only worthwhile monument is the **Chiesa di San Simplicio** (Church of San Simplicio; open 9am–1pm and 4–7pm), an unadorned Pisan Romanesque granite basilica behind the railway station.

The Gulf of Olbia is dominated by the great bulk of the **Isola Tavolara**, an uninhabited island with sandy beaches, a tiny harbour and a couple of trattorias. Summer ferries depart from the busy beach resort of Porto San Paolo south of Olbia and there are boat excursions stopping off here and at the smaller neighbouring Isola di Molara (Island of Molara).

Costa Smeralda

North of Olbia the summer traffic crawls to the Costa Smeralda. Roads branch off east to **Golfo d'Aranci** (Gulf of Crabs, not Oranges), a busy port and villa resort, and, on the peninsula to the west, the **Porto Rotondo** (Round Port). The resort doesn't quite make it geographically into the Costa Smeralda, but certainly competes, with its swish marina, chi-chi boutiques and 27-room holiday villa of Silvio Berlusconi.

The Costa Smeralda

The story goes that when the Aga Khan sailed past this small strip of remote coast in 1958 he decided it would make the perfect holiday spot. Four years later, heading a private consortium, he bought the land from local farmers. The coastline of rocky capes, sheltered coves and ravishing sandy bays was to become the most famous holiday playground in the Mediterranean. Today the hotels and bars command some of the highest prices in Europe – the Hotel Cala di Volpe is so exclusive that in high season you need celebrity status to stay there.

Although the name is often used to refer to the whole area between Olbia and Palau or even Santa Teresa Gallura, the Costa Smeralda is limited to the stretch between Cala di Petra Ruja, on the Gulf of Cugnana, and Liscia di Vacca, in the north. When the Costa was created strict rules were laid down as to its development: a limited amount of land was to be

The exclusive Cala di Volpe hotel at Porto Cervo

built upon, nothing was to be high-rise or garish, the building stone was to conform to strict specifications, any trees and plants uprooted by construction were to be replaced and all newly planted vegetation was to be indigenous to Sardinia. The regulations were adhered to and building was limited to villas and villa-style hotels, sprouting discreetly amid luxuriant gardens; **Porto Cervo**, the only resort, was created to accommodate luxurious pleasure craft and provide Milan-style boutiques and people-watching cafés. It is all undeniably tasteful, though it has to be said, somewhat contrived and prohibitively expensive.

La Piazzetta in the centre of Porto Cervo is the place to watch the fashion parade go by, preferably in the early evening. Across the beach the huge, exclusive yachting marina is one of the best equipped in the Mediterranean.

The Costa is liberally endowed with four and five-star hotels, most of which have private beaches reserved for guests. For others, beach space is at a premium. Signposting is poor and in high season you may have to park some distance from the beach. Among the loveliest **beaches** are the Poltu di li Cogghj (also known as Il Principe), Cappricioli and Liscia Rujas. Liscia di Vacca in the north is an irresistible beach of brilliant white sand, accessed via a dirt track. Beyond here, resorts become, relatively speaking, cheaper, livelier and less stylish.

Arzachena

The inland town of **Arzachena**, set amid rolling hills and vineyards, is the main centre for the Costa Smeralda. The old centre is more Sardinian than anything you'll see on the coast, particularly on market day (Wednesday) when colourful stalls spill on to the streets. Hidden in the rural surroundings of the town are the remains of **nuraghic tombs and temples** (unless otherwise stated sites are open daily in summer 9am–1pm and 4–8pm, reduced hours off-season; admission fee, cumulative tickets and guided tours available in Italian, or in English with advance notice; tel: 0789 81537).

Li Lolghi Giant's Tomb

The five sites are not easy to locate, but you can pick up a map from the tourist office 3km (2 miles) east of the town on the Olbia road. The **Nuraghe Albucciu** (open all day) is easily accessed across the road (via an underpass) from the tourist office; the **Tempietto Malchittu** is a 2km (1½ mile) walk from the office, along an idyllic country path; the small roofless temple below a mysterious rocky outcrop is thought to date from the early nuraghic period (1500–1200BC). To the west **Coddu 'Ecchju** (also called Coddu Vecchiu; open all day) and **Li Lolghi** are striking examples of 'giants' tombs' *(see page 13)*. At **Li Muri**, on a country road near Li Lolghi, the circles of stones mark the site of a major necropolis dated 3500–2700BC.

Excursions from Palau

Palau

Returning to the coast, **Palau** is a lively resort and ferry port, linked in summer to Naples, Genoa and Porto Vecchio in Corsica and all year round to the nearby islands of the Maddalena Archipelago. The stiff breezes are ideal for yachting, and **Porto Pollo** (also known as Portu Puddu), 7km (4½ miles) to the west, is a haven for windsurfers. The coastline around here is studded with remarkable wind-sculpted rock formations, including the famous **Roccia d'Orso**, a huge bear-shaped rock 6km (4 miles) east of the town, near the Capo d'Orso fort. A symbol of Palau, the bear has served as a landmark to sailors since ancient times.

West of Palau on the Porto Rafael road, the austere-looking **Fortezza di Monte Altura** (guided tours daily Apr–June and Sept–mid-Oct 10am–1pm and 3–7pm, July–Aug 9am–noon and 4–8pm; admission fee) was built in the 19th century to defend the coast, though it was never actually put to the test. Obligatory tours are in Italian only, but the main attraction is the superb view of the Maddalena Archipelago.

Arcipelago della Maddalena

According to Nelson, the anchorage between mainland Sardinia and the archipelago was 'the finest man o'war harbour in Europe'. His fleet was frequently present here in the run up to Trafalgar and he tried, unsuccessfully, to persuade the British to purchase Sardinia (they opted for Malta instead).

The archipelago consists of seven main islands and over 50 islets. In 1994 the whole area was designated a national park to safeguard the environment. The main **Isola della Maddalena** is just 20 minutes by ferry from Palau and is hugely popular in summer. The arrival point is the busy little fishing port of **La Maddalena** – a lively town, with plenty of cafés and bars to quench the thirst of the large number of Italian and American sailors at the naval base. West of town, the **Museo Archeologico Navale** (open Mon–Sat

View of Arcipelago della Maddalena

10am–1pm; admission fee) exhibits treasures from ship-wrecks, including amphoras, bronze figures and jewels recovered from a Roman vessel which capsized by the island of Spargi around AD120. The sparsely inhabited island of **Caprera**, linked to La Maddalena by a causeway, is princi-pally visited for the **Compendio Garibaldi**, the last home of the great military leader for Italian unification (open Tues–Sun 9am–1pm; admission fee). Garibaldi (1807–82) purchased part of the island, built a home for himslef here and managed to use the infertile terrain for farming, veg-etable growing and viticulture. Guided tours (usually in Ital-ian) of the Casa Bianca (White House) take in Garibaldi memorabilia including his famous red shirt, his deathbed (the clocks in the room are fixed at the time of his death) and the tomb where he was buried in 1882.

The other main islands, Budelli, Razzoli, Spargi and Santa Maria, can be visited only by boat. Excursions from La Mad-dalena (or Palau) skirt the islands and stop off at secluded beaches. The beguiling waters here are ideal for scuba div-ing or snorkelling and the islands are a paradise for private yachts. One of the loveliest beaches is Budelli's beautiful **Spiagga Rosa**, famed for the enchanting pink-tinged sands. To protect the beach, swimming here has been forbidden since 1999. The two little islands to the north, Isola Razzóli and Isola Santa Maria, are separated by the Passo degli Asinelli, named after the donkeys which used to carry pro-visions from Santa Maria to the lighthouse keeper at Razzoli when there was no quay for boats.

Santa Teresa Gallura

The far northern tip of Sardinia is buffeted by the *mistrale*, resulting in strange rock formations. The most spectacular is **Capo Testa**, the promontory of white granite boulders, west of Santa Teresa Gallura. From the lighthouse you can

Capo Testa

walk to scenic coves, including Cala dei Corsari where Roman columns can be seen on the seabed. The promontory was used as a quarry, and granite from here was used for Rome's Pantheon and Pisa's cathedral. The promontory is joined to the mainland by an isthmus lined with sandy beaches.

The nearby resort of Santa Teresa looks across to Corsica, 11km (7 miles) away. The town of Bonifacio makes a popular day trip – ferries make the crossing about eight times daily (fewer off-season). Ferries also link the resort with La Maddalena. The oldest part of the town of Santa Teresa dates from the early 1800s when King Vittorio Emanuele repopulated the then abandoned town with Piedmontese and named it after his wife, Teresa. The town expanded into a holiday resort in the 1960s. Off-season it is quiet, but come June and July the streets teem with tourists. The centre has abundant bars, trattorias and street markets creating a lively atmosphere. A fine 16th-century Spanish watchtower stands on the promontory between the port and the main beach. The central beach, Spiaggia di Rena Bianca, is packed in summer, but the beaches on the Capo Testa isthmus are less congested, as are the lovely white stretches of sand to the east of the resort.

Tempio Pausania

From Palau the *Trenino Verde* (the little green train, *see page 123*) climbs up to **Tempio Pausania**, in the wooded heart of Gallura. Far removed from the summer bustle on the coast, the region's capital lies high up in the hills, with clear mountain air, therapeutic springs and dignified streets lined with grey granite houses. South of Tempio, the mountain range of Monte Limbara rises to 1,359m (4,457ft) and its peak, **Punta Balistrieri**, affords sweeping vistas.

From Tempio a road snakes up to **Aggius**, an attractive village strikingly set among granite outcrops. The impressive **Museo Etnográfico** (Ethnographical Museum; open mid-May–mid-Oct 10am–1pm and 3–8.30pm; mid-Oct–mid-May Tues–Sun 10am–1pm and 3.30–7pm; admission fee) is devoted to local crafts and industries, ranging from bread-making and carpet-weaving to granite quarrying and cork production. Apart from its industry, Aggius is renowned for a long-standing vendetta between two local families, which resulted in 72 murders.

The Cork of Gallura

You won't have to drive far in Gallura to spot the cork oak. The tree (*Quercus suber*) is easily recognised by its twisted branches, glossy green evergreen leaves or the raw red trunk where the bark has been recently stripped. Cultivating the cork is a lengthy process. The trees must mature for 25–30 years before the first cutting of the outer layer. Skilled foresters strip off the roll of bark using special axes, leaving the tender inner layer undamaged. The bark grows again but is not ready for restripping for another nine or ten years. The process is repeated and the quality of the cork improves year by year. The virgin cork is fit only for floors, floats, life-jackets or decorative purposes: the superior cork in your champagne or wine bottle will be from the second or subsequent strippings.

ALGHERO AND THE NORTHWEST

The northwest has a host of attractions, from the charming old quarter of Alghero and the historic towns of Bosa and Castelsardo to the Pisan Romanesque churches, prehistoric *nuraghe* and stunning sands of Stintino.

Alghero

Tradition has it that the Emperor Charles V, on a visit to **Alghero** in 1541, found the city *bonita y ben asentada* – charming and well located. Over four and a half centuries later, the description still holds true. It is arguably the most appealing of Sardinia's tourist centres, with its picturesque medieval core and its coast of white beaches and glorious azure waters.

Set on the northwest coast, the town appropriately faces the Iberian Peninsula, which played such a major role in its

Alghero's historic centre

history. In 1353 the Aragonese overthrew the Genoese who had founded a fortress here in the early Middle Ages; the local Sardinians and Ligurians fled, and the town was repopulated with Catalans. Alghero became part of the Kingdom of Aragon and remained in Spanish hands for four centuries. Still today it retains marked Spanish characteristics, not only in the architecture of its monuments but in the Catalan street names (alongside Italian ones), the archaic form of the Catalan language which is still spoken here and the Catalan-style seafood dishes that are served in many restaurants.

The population of 45,000 more than doubles in summer and the number of visitors continues to rise with the boom in cheap flights to Fertilia airport. But tourism has not spoiled Alghero's charm. It is a fishing port as well as a tourist centre, and unlike most Sardinian resorts, stays alive all year.

The city can easily be covered on foot and the pedestrianised streets of the centre make for pleasant strolling. The beautifully preserved **Centro Storico** (Historic Centre) comprises a network of narrow cobbled alleys, flanked by mellow stone houses. The Catalan architectural influence can be seen in some of the carved portals and windows with Gothic arches. The perimeter of the old town is marked on

What's in a Name?

Scholars are divided on the derivation of the name Alghero. The original name was S'Alighera and the most accredited hypothesis (though not the most popular locally) is that it comes from the Latin *algae*, or seaweed – which off-season still invades the shores. The name could also come from the Arabic *Al Gar* meaning cave, alluding to the Grotta di Nettuno (Neptune's Cave). The name *S'Alighera* was later changed to *Algarium*, and then by the Aragonese to the Catalan *L'Alguer* – the name still used in local dialect.

Chiesa di San Francesco

three sides by the old city walls and the sturdy towers embedded within them. At sunset the sea-facing *bastioni* or ramparts are the venue of the summer *passegiata* (evening stroll). But at any time of day a walk along the walls affords wonderful views.

Via Carlo Alberto is the busiest and most elegant of the main arteries, lined by small shops selling crafts, clothes and coral jewellery. The **Chiesa di San Francesco** (Church of San Francesco; open daily 9am–noon and 5–8pm) is a notable landmark with a Gothic campanile and attractive cloister (accessed via the sacristy) where concerts are held in summer. At the end of Via Carlo Alberto the multicoloured majolica-tiled dome of the Church of San Michele is a conspicuous landmark and symbol of Alghero. The **Cattedrale di Santa Maria** (Cathedral of Santa Maria; open daily 7am–noon and 5–7.30pm; off-season Mon–Fri 7am–1pm and 3.30–6.30pm, Sat 7am–noon and 3.30–6.30pm) on Piazza Duomo is a hodgepodge of styles. An ostentatious, neoclassical façade belies a Renaissance interior with baroque chapels and an elaborate carved altarpiece and pulpit. The beautiful Catalan-Gothic belltower, with a fine sculpted portal, is easily missed in Via Principe Umberto behind the church (guided visits June–Sept Tues–Thur and Sat 7pm–9.30pm; admission fee).

Riviera del Corallo and Grotta di Nettuno

The **Riviera del Corallo**, west of Alghero, is named after the coral reefs at the foot of the limestone cliffs. The finest beaches, Le Bombarde and Lazzaretto, lie beyond Fertilia, the soulless town created by the Fascists in 1936 as part of a large land-reclamation programme. The bay of **Porto Conte**, where some of Algerho's smartest hotels hide among the pines, is a large natural harbour fringed with sandy bays. The panoramic coast road takes you south to **Capo Caccia**, the imposing limestone promontory formerly used for game shooting and today a haunt of the herring gull and (more rarely) the peregrine falcon. Just before the tip of the promontory a side road leads to the Escala del Cabirol, a dramatic stairway of 656 steps descending 110m (360ft) to the entrance of the **Grotta di Nettuno** (Neptune's Grotto; open 8am–7pm, off-season 9am–2pm, guided tours on the hour; admission fee), the most spectacular of Sardinia's caves. Since the first mention of this fairytale cavern in the 18th century, writers and travellers have extolled its virtues. One of them was the English barrister, John Tyndale, who likened it to the Alhambra. In the 19th century, sailors used to illuminate the deep cave with hundreds of candles and at one time it became the setting for candlelit concerts (today it's lit by electricity).

Boat to the grotto

A less strenuous way of reaching the Grotta di Nettuno *(below)* is by excursion boat from Alghero. This scenic trip takes two to three hours; the entrance fee to the cave is not included.

Archaeological Sites

Roughly halfway between Alghero and Capo Caccia, a layby provides an excellent view of the **Nuraghe di Palmavera** (open daily Apr–Oct 9am–7pm, Nov–Feb until 2pm, March until 4.30pm; admission fee), a fortified nuraghic village which was abandoned in the 5th century BC. The remains comprise the principal and original limestone tower (1500–900BC), the secondary tower, ramparts and the 'Meeting Hut' (900–800BC), and the 50 or so circular village dwellings, added in the final phase (800–700BC). To the north, on the Alghero/Porto Torres road, the **Necropoli di Anghelu Ruju** (Anghelu Ruju Necropolis; same openings as Nuraghe di Palmavera; cumulative ticket available) is an extensive complex of 36 burial chambers, known as *domus de janas* and dating from the late Neolithic era (3300–2900BC). The size of some of the tombs suggests collective burials and the finds, including female idols, bowls and deposits of shells, mixed with ash and charcoal, are evidence of funerary rituals and feasts.

Near the necropolis is the smart **Sella and Mosca** wine estate, surrounded by lush gardens and 500 hectares (135 acres) of vineyards. They produce a whole range of wines, and free guided tours (June–Oct at 5.30pm) take in the cellars, museum and a film on the history of the estate. The Enoteca (wine shop) is open all year for the sale of wines.

Bosa

South of Alghero the coastal road curves along the wild rocky shore and cuts through hills carpeted in clumps of gorse and euphorbia – a spectacular riot of yellow in late spring. Near Capo Maragiu watch out for griffon vultures circling above – this is home to the largest colony in Italy of these rare birds.

In the valley of the River Remo and surrounded by mountains, **Bosa** feels quite remote. The **Castello Malaspina** (Malaspina Castle; open daily 10am–1pm, afternoon hours

Bosa and the River Temo

dependent on season; admission fee) towers above the town and is evidence of Bosa's importance as a medieval city. It was built on the hill as a fortress in the 12th century, though only the walls and towers survive. Within the castle the little 14th–15th century Church of Nostra Signora di Regnos Altos shelters a remarkable 14th-century cycle of frescoes. The castle ramparts command fine views of the mountains, sea and town. Huddled below is the old town of **Sa Costa**, a maze of alleys and picturesquely tumbledown houses. On the left bank of the Temo lie the abandoned tanning buildings of the **Sas Conzas** quarter. Bosa was famous for cowhide and throughout the 18th century had a thriving trade selling to Genoa and France. Nineteenth-century travellers who praised the beauty of Bosa invariably made mention of the foul smells of the tanneries and river. These came from the mixture of water and dog excrement used to purge the skins and give them greater elasticity. A museum here tells the story of the industry.

Malvasia di Bosa

Look out for the rich, amber-coloured Malvasia di Bosa, sold in wine cellars and shops, and served in all Bosa's restaurants.

The **Cattedrale di San Pietro Extramuros** (open daily 10am–1pm and 3.30–6pm), Bosa's former cathedral, lies isolated 2km (1½ miles) upstream. Formerly part of a Cistercian monastery, it is a simple and evocative Romanesque church with a Gothic façade. The present-day counterpart is the **Cattedrale dell'Immacolata**, a very different rococo-style church on the Corso Vittorio Emanuele II. This main thoroughfare running through the centre was home to the wealthy bourgeoisie and is lined by elegant houses. A good example is the restored **Casa Deriu** at No. 59 (open Tues–Sun 10am– 1pm and 4–6pm; admission fee). Small cavernous shops occupy the lower floors of some of the houses.

Sássari

This is the principal city of northern Sardinia and the second largest on the island after Cágliari. Despite being a busy commercial centre, surrounded by unsightly swathes of industry, it's an attractive place to observe Sardinian town life. It also has an old quarter of medieval streets and the second best archaeological museum on the island.

Sássari developed as a medieval town when Saracen raids on the coast forced the inhabitants to retreat from the sea. Pisan rulers were followed by Catalan Aragonese, who controlled the city for four centuries. In the 16th century the Jesuits established Sardinia's first university here, and the city is generally regarded as the intellectual capital of the island. It is also famous for its festivals: the **Cavalcata Sarda**, featuring an equestrian parade and frenzied horseracing and the **Festa dei Candelieri** when local guilds bear huge wooden candles in a procession along Corso Vittorio Emanuele II.

The town's hub is **Piazza d'Italia**, a spacious, stately square, with central, palm-shaded gardens. The east side is flanked by the neoclassical Palazzo della Provincia (Town Hall). In the early evenings Sassaresi can be seen en masse strolling in the piazza or taking aperitifs at one of the bars under the colonnades on the northwest side of the square.

Going up from Piazza d'Italia, the Via Roma is home to Sássari's most elegant shops, as well as a useful tourist office and, at No. 64, the **Museo Nazionale Sanna** (Sanna National Museum; open daily Tues–Sun 9am–2pm; admission fee). The impressive archaeological collection ranges from the Neolithic to the Roman, and encompasses Phoenician and Carthaginian finds. An extensive nuraghic section displays reconstructions of sanctuaries and some superb little bronzes, including warriors with weapons and boats with bull-head prows.

Roman mosaics in the Museo Nazionale Sanna

In the heart of the old town, the **Duomo di San Nicola** (Cathedral of San Nicola) rears up from its small square, the extravagant Spanish baroque façade incongruously fronting an otherwise Gothic structure. This was built by the Spanish over a Romanesque church. It's well worth exploring the *vincoli* (narrow alleys) around the church with their cavernous stores, little local restaurants and occasional artisan workshop. On the other side of Corso Vittorio Emanuele II, **Piazza Tola** is a charming little square and scene of a daily morning market.

Basilica della Santissima Trinità di Saccargia

Sardinia's most famous Romanesque church makes quite an impact as you hurtle along the Sássari–Olbia highway. Isolated in a valley 16km (10 miles) southeast of the city, the church (open daily summer 9am–8pm, spring and autumn 9am–dusk; admission fee) has an eye-catching black and white striped façade and a soaring belltower. Built by the Pisans in the 11th century, it once formed part of a large monastic complex. The name *Saccargia* means dappled cow in Sardinian dialect – the valley was pastureland and there are depictions of carved cows among the sculpted decorations in the porch. The interior is simple and evocative, and the central apse is enhanced by a beautiful cycle of frescoes by a Pisan master – the only existing cycle of 13th-century frescoes in Sardinia.

The Saccargia church is just one of the Pisan Romanesque jewels in the region, all easily reached from the SS597: the abandoned **San Michele di Salvenero**, 3km (2 miles) southeast of the Saccargia church; the brown and black basalt **Santa Maria del Regno**, dominating the hilltop village of Ardara, with a huge and elaborate early 16th-century *retablo* over the altar; and the beautiful **Sant'Antioco di Bisárcio** near Ozieri – once a cathedral, now completely isolated.

Ozieri

The town has lent its name to the Ozieri Culture, dating from 4th and 3rd millennia BC when the first villages were established on the island. Finds from this era, including ceramics and statuettes, were discovered in the Grotta di San Michele (Grotto of San Michele) on the outskirts of Ozieri and can be seen in the small **Museo Archeologico** (Archaeological

Museum; open Tues–Sat 9am–1pm and 4–7pm, Sun 9.30am–12.30pm; admission fee) in Piazza San Francesco. The Grotto itself is also open to the public but is of limited interest. Little survives of old Ozieri, but the town enjoys a fine setting, its houses and apartments stacked up on the valley slopes.

Valle dei Nuraghi

The region southwest of Ozieri, strewn with the remains of ancient civilisations, has been dubbed the 'Valley of the *Nuraghi*'. If you only have time for one of them, make it **Nuraghe Santu Antine**, about 4km (2½ miles) south of Torralba and easy to get to from the main SS131 (open daily 9am–sunset; admission fee). The *nuraghe* was built and inhabited between the 15th and 9th centuries BC. The oldest section is the massive central keep, standing at 17.5m (57ft) – originally it was around 22m (72ft) with a third storey. The

Valle dei Nuraghi

tower is surrounded by a three-sided rampart, incorporating three secondary towers. Scant remains of villages, from Nuraghic to Carthaginian and Roman, lie outside the walls. Torralba's archaeological museum contains finds from the site and a small-scale model of the nuraghe.

North Coast

Porto Torres or Turris Libisonis was founded by the Romans in 27BC and became a major trading centre with temples, thermal baths, basilicas and splendid villas. Today it is essentially an industrial ferry port, whose oil refineries, petrochemical works and unsightly outskirts deter all but the most dedicated sightseers. The **Basilica di San Gavino** (Basilica of San Gavino; open daily 8.30am–1pm and 3–7pm; admission fee) is a beautiful example of Pisan Romanesque architecture and the largest Romanesque church of its type in Sardinia. Now swamped by modern development, it is hard to imagine that it once stood in an open rural landscape. The church is dedicated to Saints Gavino, Proto and Gianuario who were all beheaded in AD304 for converting to Christianity. The saints are commemorated by wooden statues within the church and sarcophagi with their remains

San Gavino

in the lower crypt. The Roman marble columns inside the church suggest there was a temple on or near the site.

Near the railway station just back from the seafront, the **Antiquarium Turritano** (open Tues–Sun 9am–8pm, in high season until 11pm; admission fee) testifies to the importance of the Roman colony (formerly called Turris Libisonis). Visits start with the excellent archaeological museum, housing Roman finds, and continue to the archaelogical site known as the *Palazzo del Re Bárbaro*, the palace of the Roman governor Barbarus. The site includes the remains of the Roman public baths, mosaic floors, roads and shops.

Between Sássari and Porte Torres, and marked off the main SS131, the sanctuary of **Monte d'Accoddi** (open daily 9am–6pm, winter until 5pm; admission fee) is a rare sacred mound left by the pre-nuraghic Ozieri Culture *(see page 76)*. The high pyramidal mound, flattened at the top, is surrounded by high walls of limestone blocks and has a ramp leading up to what was some form of altar or shrine.

Stintino

On a narrow windswept peninsula at the northwest tip of Sardinia, Stintino was formerly no more than a peaceful fishing village. It still is off season, but in summer tourists pour in for the beautiful beaches, seafood restaurants and the hotels and villas that have sprouted up by the beach.

The village was founded by 45 families of fishermen and farmers who were exiled from the neighbouring island of **Asinara** in 1885 when the government turned Asinara into a penal colony and quarantine station. The prison closed in 1994 and today the 17-km (10½-mile) long, windswept island is an uninhabited national park, with unpolluted beaches, mouflons (long-horned wild sheep) and white donkeys *(asini)*, after which the island is named. From Easter to September excursions to the island depart from Stintino and Porto Torres (numbers are limited to 500 a day). For information contact Stintours (tel: 0795 23160; <www.stintours.com>).

In Stintino's picturesque old port, lateen sailing boats sit side by side with fishing boats and pleasure craft. The prime attraction is the **Pelosa beach**, 4km (2½ miles) to the north, a Caribbean-like expanse of fine white sands, lapped by blue-green waters. Offshore a ruined Aragonese watchtower dominates the island of Piana – with Isola Asinara beyond.

Stintino used to be a major tuna fishing centre, renowned for the annual *mattanza* or tuna massacre *(see page 38)*. Near the new port, the **Museo della Tonnara** (Tonnara Museum; open June–mid-Sept evenings only 6–11pm; admission fee) demonstrates through film, video and marine memorabilia the methods of netting and killing the fish. The practice was abandoned in 1974, by which time the tuna migration routes had changed and the high-cost traditional fishing rituals could no longer compete with new techniques.

Castelsardo

The SS200 follows the coast east of Porto Torres to **Castelsardo**, a fortress village which perches picturesquely on a high

Elephant Rock

The famous and much-photographed Roccia dell'Elefante (Elephant Rock) stands 4km (2½ miles) southeast of Castelsardo, at the intersection of the SS200 and SS134. The wind-sculpted elephant hides the ancient remains of rock-cut tombs known as *domus de janas*.

rocky promontory. Over the centuries the name has been changed according to the colonisers: from the early 12th century, when the Genoese established a castle here, it was Castel Genovese, from the mid-15th century Castel Aragonese and since the mid-18th century (when Sardinia became part of the House of Savoy), Castelsardo. The heavily renovated **castle** was inhabited by the illustrious Dorian family, and is thought to have been the home of Eleonora of Arborea *(see page 16)* and her Genoese husband, Brancaleone Doria, for around 10 years. The castle terraces command splendid sea views, stretching as far as Corsica on a clear day. The castle houses the **Museo dell'Intreccio** (Museum of Basket-weaving; open high season daily 9.30am–midnight, off-season 9am–1pm and 3pm–dusk, closed Mon in winter; admission fee). Castelsardo is a long-established centre for basketry made from dwarf palm leaves, reeds and asphodel.

Picturesque Castelsardo

Basket-weaving was formerly the occupation of almost every female in town, from young girls to grandmothers.

The town manages to retain its charm despite the large numbers of tourists. Tightly packed houses and small shops selling handicrafts and souvenirs cluster at the foot of the fortress and old ladies weaving baskets can still sometimes be seen in the doorways of tiny alleys. The **Cattedrale di Sant'Antonio Abate** (Cathedral of Sant'Antonio Abate) perches precariously on the rocks, conspicuous by its fine – majolica-tiled cupola. The altar is graced by the 15th century painting of *Madonna con gli Angeli* (Madonna with Angels), by the Maestro di Castelsardo – a much-admired Spanish-influenced artist about whom little is known.

WHAT TO DO

ENTERTAINMENT

Nightlife

For action after dark you should head for the late-night bars or clubs *(discoteche)* in the capital, other main towns or the more lively coastal resorts where discos in summer are open until the early hours of the morning. The town of Alghero is lively by night, the streets of the historic centre lined by open-air bars. For the large nightclubs you need to head 10km (6 miles) out of the city after midnight, either to La Siesta at Locolità Monte Ladu on the SS292 (open summer only, 1–6am) on the Villanova road, or Ruscello Disco Club (open from midnight) on the Olmedo road.

Theatre and Music

Cágliari's Anfiteatro Romano (Roman Amphitheatre) is a dramatic setting for summer drama, dance performances or rock concerts. In the high season ancient sites such as Tharros and Noro host theatre, opera and concert performances. Movie aficionadas will find cinemas in the main towns, but films are rarely in their original language. For listings, consult local newspapers or visit the tourist office.

SHOPPING

The island has seen a revival in traditional handicrafts. Some of the craftwork is beautifully made, decorated with designs based on Punic and even earlier symbolic patterns. Along with authentic crafts comes the inevitable kitsch and imita-

Ceramics from Dorgali

Making lobster pots

tion goods, from mock coral to fake Gucci bags sold by hawkers on piazzas and beaches. (Note that fines of up to €10,000 are imposed on shoppers caught buying counterfeit goods.) To see the genuine Sardinian article head for the shops that belong to the Istituto Sardo Organizzazione Lavoro Artigianale, or ISOLA – a government-sponsored organisation set up to safeguard the island's craftwork traditions. Prices are on the high side but at least authenticity is guaranteed. The products come from local crafts cooperatives and include carpets, rugs, wall hangings, tapestries, embroidery, basketry, ceramics, wood-carvings, leatherwork, cork, and gold filigree jewellery, often worked with coral. The Cágliari branch is at Via Bacaredda 176. Sássari has an exhibition of Sardinian handicrafts at the Padiglione dell'Artigianato Sardo in the public gardens. You can sometimes buy direct from the source, particularly in villages where locals display their home-made crafts.

Antiques and Curios

Antiques and curio markets are held in Cágliari's Piazza del Carmine on the first Sunday of the month, in Piazza Carlo Alberto on the second and fourth Sundays and flea markets are held on Sundays on the Bastione St Remy (August excepted). Handmade shepherds' knives, both antique and modern, are widely sold; those with hand-carved horn handles are the most valuable. The main knife-making centre is the village of Pattada in the province of Sássari, and the knives are known as *pattades*. Other popular souvenirs are replicas of little bronze nuraghic figures.

Basketware

Basketmaking is a centuries-old craft. In the Campidano area local women still make baskets from dwarf palm leaves and rush, which are then decorated with strips of red cloth to create traditional designs. In the province of Nuoro, asphodel is used to make mats and baskets. In Castelsardo you can still see women weaving baskets on the steps of their houses in the streets of the old town. Samples of locally made basketware, from food containers to lobster pots, can be seen in the Museum of Wickerwork within Castelsardo's castle.

Clothes and Accessories

For Italian designerware, Sardinian towns can't compare with the shopping meccas of the mainland, but Cágliari has some smart boutiques and, for those with well-lined wallets, the Costa Smeralda has an abundance of designer labels and chic jewellers. For Italian designerware try Cágliari's Via Manno, between Bastione di San Remy and Piazza

Myrtle liqueur

A favourite souvenir of Sardinia is a cork-wrapped bottle of *liquore di mirto*, distilled from the berries of myrtle plants that proliferate on hillsides.

Yenne, and Largo Carlo Felice. Via Roma, facing the water-front, has some elegant boutiques and is also home to La Rina-scente, the island's main department store, selling high-quality clothes and accessories (open Mon–Sat 9am–8.30pm, Sun 10am–9pm). In Alghero the main shopping street is Via Carlo Alberto, with clothes boutiques and jewellery shops.

Food and Wine

Look out for signs on the roadside for cheeses, hams, smoked meats, olive oil, honey or liqueurs. *Agriturismi* (farming properties offering accommodation) often sell homemade produce. Cágliari's Marina quarter (the streets behind the main Via Roma) have specialist food shops with a wide sel-ection of pecorino and other cheeses, as well as wild boar ham, smoked meats, sea urchin paté, local wines and spirits. Sapori di Sardegna at Via Campidano 1/c (on the corner of

Quality leatherwork from Dorgali

Via Roma) offers the whole range of Sardinian specialities: *bottarga* (dried mullet roe) from Cabras, *carta di musica* (flat crisp Sardinian bread), piquant *pecorino* cheeses and *filu e ferru* (the local firewater).

On Piazza Yenne the Pasticceria Antonio Deplano has a wonderful array of pastries, sweets and cakes made of marzipan, almonds and figs. The Mercato Coperto di San Benedetto at Via Cocco Ortu (open Mon–Fri mornings, Sat all day) is the longest indoor market in Italy, with a wonderful array of fish, cheeses, hams and other regional specialities.

In Alghero Dolce e Piccante at Vicolo Buragna 4 stocks the best Sardinian wines along with salamis, cheeses and *dolci*. If you're killing time before a flight home from Alghero's Fertilia airport, drop in to the nearby Enoteca (wine shop) at the Sella and Mosca Estate *(see page 72)* for a wide range of wines. In the Barbagia region, Tonara is renowned for *torrone*, a type of nougat sold throughout the island.

Jewellery
Delicate gold and silver filigree, as worn with traditional Sardinian costumes, is made by local jewellers; this is often combined with coral to make earrings, necklaces, bracelets and rings. Alghero's streets have many coral shops, though little of it comes from the depleted reefs on its Riviera del Corallo.

Textiles and Ceramics
The best buys are hand-woven carpets, rugs and wall hangings, often decorated with geometrical patterns, cotton tablecloths, embroidery, linen and lace. Dorgali in Nuoro province is a major centre for handicrafts, particularly for carpets, embroidered shawls, ceramics, jewellery and leather. Specific to the region are the large triangular 'shepherds' bags' sold in leather shops. Ceramics, sold all over the island, range from traditional terracotta ware to innovative modern vases and bowls.

CHILDREN'S SARDINIA

Italians are indulgent towards children and Sardinians are no exception. They will always be made to feel welcome, and are readily accepted in restaurants. Although there are few attractions specifically designed for youngsters, the island offers sandy, gently shelving beaches with idyllic seas for swimming and a wide range of water sports. Most families opt for a resort and stay put, deterred by the long distances (often along hairpin bends) between main towns and resorts. The majority of coastal hotels have their own pools with a separate paddling section for youngsters. Some of the larger establishments lay on entertainment for children of all ages.

Beaches and Boat Trips

Main beaches have water sports facilities as well as pedaloes, canoes and banana boats. For a change of scenery try one of the boat excursions. Popular trips are the Maddalena Archipelago, either on a day's organised excursion or by ferry from Palau; the island of Tavorola east of Olbia; and the pristine beaches on Nuoro's east coast, accessible by boat from Cala Gonone.

Fun Parks

The Aquadream water park at Baia Sardinia (open mid-June–mid-Sept 10am–6pm, tel: 0789 99511) offers swimming pools, chutes and other aquatic activities. Water Paradise north of Sorso in Sássari province, off the Porto Torres–Castelsardo road (open June–Sept 10am–7pm, tel: 0793 67016) offers similar facilities. At Sardinia in Miniature in the village of Tuili (tel: 0709 361004) you can stroll through all the island's main monuments. The village is close to Barumini and a trip could be combined with Su Nuraxi (see page 42).

Sightseeing

Unless your child is a budding archaeologist, interest in the prehistoric nuraghic stone cones and archaeological museums is bound to wane after a while. More appealing are hilltop castles, grottoes and catacombs. Of the main towns, Alghero has the most to offer: a relaxed place with car-free alleys, seafront walks, medieval towers, a lively port and exciting boat trips to the Grotta di Nettuno *(see page 71)*. The Aquarium, though not spectacular, has more than 100 species of fish.

Jogging on the beach

SPORTS

With 1,800km (1,125 miles) of coastline and clear blue waters, Sardinia is ideal for all types of watersports. The offshore winds make it a haven for sailing and windsurfing, and the sea is ideal for swimming and scuba diving. Recent years have seen a surge in other outdoor pursuits, from hiking and biking to tree climbing and caving. *Agriturismi* (holiday farms) often provide opportunities for exploring the countryside, on horseback, by bike or on foot.

Cycling

Hiring a bike is a great way of exploring the island, though the hills and mountains make for some strenuous pedalling.

Mountain-bike holidays, either group or self-guided tours, are becoming increasingly popular. Overnight stays are often in local *agriturismi*. For information contact Dolce Vita Bike Tours (<www.dolcevitabiketours.com>). Most of the large towns and coastal resorts hire out mountain bikes. Tourist offices can provide details of bike rental locations, along with recommended cycling routes.

Golf

The most prestigious golf courses on the island are the Pevero Golf Club (18 holes) at Cala di Volpe, Costa Smeralda, tel: 0789 958000, created by Robert Trent Jones in 1972 and the Is Molas Golf Club (18 holes) at Santa Margherita di Pula, Cágliari, tel: 0709 241006. The third 18-hole course is the Is Arenas Golf and Country Club on the west coast, tel: 0783 52036. There are nine-hole courses at Sássari, San Teodoro, Mirana and Villasimius.

Climbing in the Gennargentu

Hiking and Climbing

Sardinia has some stunning walking country, especially the Sopramonte in the Barbagia region and the Gennargentu mountains. But hiking in the interior is a relatively recent pursuit, and facilities are limited. More tracks are being created, but don't expect a neat network

of established and marked
paths. Many hikers hire the
services of a local guide.
Local tourist offices can
provide details, or you can
find information from the
*Guide Ambientali Escur-
sionistiche* at <www.gae.it>.

Skiing Sardinia

Sardinia has one ski resort
at Fonni in the Gennargentu
mountains. At 1,000m
(3,280ft) it's the island's
highest village, but there
is no guarantee of snow.

Heavy shoes are recommended, along with thick socks to
give you protection from the thorny *macchia*. Experienced
walkers will enjoy the wild Su Gorroppu gorge in the Supramonte. The trail takes two days and requires special equip-
ment for the vertical walls of the gorge. More demanding
still is the Selvaggio Blue Route, a stunning coastal route
from Cala Luna to Santa Maria Navarrese, involving rock
climbing and abseiling. For detailed descriptions of hiking (and biking) trails and downloadable maps visit <www.
sardiniahikeandbike.com>.

Horse-riding

Horses are very much part of Sardinia's culture, and several
of the island's festivals preserve traditions of jousting and
horse-racing. Dozens of equestrian centres have sprouted on
the island, especially near Cágliari, and in the provinces of
Oristano and Nuoro. Schools offer riding lessons for all
levels, as well as excursions either along the coast or through
forests, farms and mountains. The leading equestrian centre
is at the Ala Birdi complex, on the coast at Arborea in the
province of Oristano (see <www.alabirdi.com>).

Sailing

Wind conditions off Sardinia are ideal for sailing, whether
it's a hired dinghy from a local beach or a private yacht
cruising the Costa Smeralda. Inexperienced sailors should

beware of variable winds and strong currents along the coast. The island hosts major sailing events, such as the World Championship in September. Numerous ports, marinas and landings are dotted around the Sardinian coast, but permission is usually required for mooring. The best-equipped and most exclusive port is Porto Cervo on the Costa Smeralda. *Gommoni* (rubber dinghies) can be rented from many of the beaches, and those with cash to spare can charter motorboats or sailing boats, with or without crew. Alternatively, there are plenty of boat excursions from the coastal resorts.

Scuba Diving and Snorkelling

The great clarity of the water and the numerous coves and grottoes are favourable for scuba diving and snorkelling. The island provides excellent facilities for divers of all stan-

Clear water at La Maddalena

dards and there are dozens of diving centres, many of them located on the north and northwest coast. The Alghero region alone has around 20 centres; other popular areas are Stintino on the northwest tip of the island, the Arcipelago della Maddalena in the north, the Golfo di Orosei on the east coast and the Isola di San Pietro in the southwest. Diving centres offer a whole range of possibilities, ranging from a single dive off the seashore to day trips, night dives, underwater photography and excursions to shipwrecks.

Windsurfing near Cágliari

Swimming

Sardinia's crystalline waters and pristine beaches offer some of the best swimming in the Mediterranean. Easily accessible beaches are inevitably packed in July and August; at other times of year you can usually find towel space if you're prepared to drive along (unsigned) dirt tracks, hire a boat or go for a long hike. Hotels frequently have their own beach facilities, but rarely include them in the room rate.

Windsurfing

Windsurfing is hugely popular in Sardinia and the conditions are perfect, especially on the bays of the north coast. Boards can be hired on the majority of beaches and many hotels will supply them. The most favourable spots in the north are La Maddalena, Santa Teresa di Gallura, Porto

Pollo west of Palau and La Pelosa north of Stintino; in the south popular spots are the island of Sant'Antióco, Capo Spartivento and Poetto beach near Cágliari.

FESTIVALS AND SEASONAL EVENTS

Virtually every village and town finds an excuse for a festival and over a thousand are celebrated every year on the island. It may be a *sagre*, a religious celebration in honour of a saint, a pagan ritual celebrating the season or one of the major events that draw participants from all corners of the island. Whatever the occasion the wine flows and the food is abundant. For the main festivals locals dress in exquisitely embroidered costumes and take part in major parades; some of the best-known ones involve feats of horsemanship and frenetic *Palio*-like races. But there are also less formal, rural festivals, focusing perhaps on some small country church where locals participate in a service, tuck into a huge meal at trestle tables, then dance off the calories to the accompaniment of an accordian.

Opposite is a list of the island's major festivals. Local tourist offices will provide you with information on other events. If you happen to be in Alghero on the Saturday night before Carnival, head for the Via Carmine for the Festa della Cantina, Festival of the Wine Cellars. Through the night, owners of cellars in the street offer wine and food specialities to all and sundry, creating a lively party atmosphere.

Carnival mask

Calendar of Events

16 and 17 January Feast of Sant'Antonio Abate is celebrated in towns throughout the island, the festivities revolving around huge bonfires.

February Carnival is celebrated throughout the island during the week before Shrove Tuesday. Masks, costumes, loud music, song and dance are all part of the scene. Mamoiada's festival (which also takes place on 16 and 17 January) features the procession of the red-waist-coated *Issohadores* (the hunters) and the black-masked *Mamuthones* (the hunted). Oristano hosts the *Sa Sartiglia*, a medieval equestrian pageant *(see page 45)*.

March–April Holy Week is marked by religious processions, Passion plays and street celebrations. Castelsardo is renowned for its Easter Monday *Lunissanti*, when a procession of white-hooded men winds its way through the town, to the accompaniment of chants. Oliena is famous for its Easter festivals, with processions on Good Friday and Easter Sunday. Other major events take place in Alghero, Sássari, Castelsardo and Ittireddu.

1–4 May In Cágliari's Festa di Sant'Efisio, an effigy of the saint is paraded from the Chiesa di Sant'Efisio as far as Pula and Nora, then back to the city.

Penultimate Sunday in May (Ascension Day) Sássari celebrates the *Cavalcata Sarda* with parades, dance, poetry and music, culminating in horse races, with knights in historical costume.

24 June San Giovanni Battista: the summer solstice is marked by festivities and bonfires in several towns and villages.

6–8 July The S'Ardia at Sédilo is Sardinia's equivalent to Sienna's *Il Palio* – three days of daredevil horse-racing.

14 August *I Candelieri*, held in thanksgiving to the Madonna for saving the Sassaresi from the plague in the 16th century, is named after the huge candles that are paraded through Sássari.

Penultimate or last Sunday of August Nuoro's major Festa del Redentore features colourful parades and folk dancing displays.

Last Sunday of October Aritzo, in the heart of the island, celebrates the *Sagra delle Castagne* or chestnut harvest.

25 December Processions take place in the lead up to Christmas (Natale), but the day itself is a low-key family event.

EATING OUT

Contrary to the assumption of a good few foreigners, the island's name has nothing to do with sardines. The surrounding waters are rich in fish, but Sardinia is not traditionally a seafaring island, and its culinary traditions are meat-rather than fish-based. Typical Sard cuisine is rustic and hearty: roast suckling pig and game, thick and filling soups, pasta with rich meat sauces. Eating out on the island rarely disappoints. The quality is good, the helpings generous (often huge) and the prices fair. Each region has its specialities, whether it's sun-dried mullet roe from Cabras, *zuppa quatta* (a bread and cheese soup) from Gallura or roasted snails from Sássari. Colonisers of the island left their culinary mark, as in the *paella* and other Catalan dishes of Alghero and the Ligurian and Tunisian flavours on the island of San Pietro. Fish naturally predominates along the coast, and menus offer a good range of seafood or simply grilled or baked whole fish. If you are lucky it will be the morning's catch; but as Mediterranean supplies dwindle, frozen fish – caught a long way from Sardinian shores – increasingly become the norm.

When to eat

The locals tend to eat lunch (pranzo) from around 12.30–1 to 3pm and dinner (cena) 8–10pm or later. Most restaurants close one day a week, and this is often Monday when the fish markets are closed. However, closing days are staggered so you can always find somewhere open.

WHERE TO EAT

Traditionally *ristoranti* or restaurants are smarter and more expensive than trattorias, but these days there is little difference between the two. Like the rest of Italy, Sardinia has a proliferation of pizzerias, which are less expensive than restaurants and popular with families. The best ones use wood-fired ovens *(forno a legna)* but apart from Sundays, these are only open in the evenings. Some pizzerias double up as trattorias, offering three-course meals as well as pizzas. In the towns you can often find places serving cheap slices of pizza *(al taglio)*. *A tavola calda* is a self-service or take-away, serving pasta, risottos, meat and vegetable dishes. The settings are unremarkable but costs are cut by the absence of service and cover charge. If all you want is a snack, stop at a bar or café. To avoid service charge, avoid the terrace with waiter-service and stand at the bar for *panini* (bread rolls with fillings) or *tramezzini* (crustless sandwiches, often with very generous fillings).

Al fresco in Alghero

WHAT TO EAT

In the Italian rather than Sardinian tradition, restaurant menus will offer a choice of *antipasti* (starters). This is likely to include a selection of cold meats such as local salamis, mountain hams and seasoned sausages, local sheep's cheeses and olives. Fish starters normally feature a seafood salad, dried mullet or tuna roe or smoked fish. Some places serve an *antipasto misto* (mixed starter) from a table, buffet-style, which can be a meal in itself.

Il primo is the first course, that is, pasta or soup, which

Seafood and pasta

comes before *il secondo,* the meat or fish dish. Sardinian pasta comes in all shapes and sizes, is often home-made and is served with a wide range of sauces. Frequently found island specialities are *malloreddus* (also called *gnocchetti*), saffron-flavoured shell-shaped pasta, which is often served *alla campidanese* (with a spicy sausage and tomato sauce) and *culurgiones,* large ravioli stuffed with potato purée, egg, mint, garlic and cheese, served in a tomato or meat sauce. Another favourite is *fregula,* a *couscous*-like pasta served with clams or used in soups. Most menus offer a range of seafood pastas, typically *alla bottarga* (with mullet roe, garlic and olive oil), *ai ricci* (with sea urchins), *alle arselle* (with clams) or *all'aragosta,* with spiny lobster. *Zuppa di pesce* (fish soup) is usually excellent, but often has to be ordered in advance. *Sa Cassola* is a Spanish-influenced soup with fish, shellfish tomatoes and white wine; *zuppa di frutti di mare* or seafood soup is likely to include clams, muscles and prawns.

In the south you'll find the Ligurian-influenced *burrida* made here with *gattucci di mare* or 'little sea cats', which are in fact dogfish, marinaded and cooked with parsley, garlic, ground walnuts and vinegar.

Main Courses

Sardinia's best known meat dish is *porchetto* (also called *porcetto* and *porceddu*) – suckling pig. Traditionally, a young pig is gently roasted on a spit, flavoured with myrtle, rosemary, laurel and sage, and served on cork trays with *pane carasau (see page 101)* and leaves of myrtle. At best it's succulent and meaty, at worst tough and gristly. *Capretto* (kid goat) is done in the same way, though it's not quite as common. Goat is also used to make a rich casserole, cooked with

Entrails and Rotten Cheese

Sardinian cuisine caters for many tastes and not all the local dishes will appeal to outsiders. Don't be surprised to find horse or donkey steak (*bistecche di cavallo* or *asinello*) on the menu or restaurants where the older locals are relishing the innards of calf, veal, lamb, goat or suckling pig. Visitors with adventurous tastes might like to try some of the traditional specialities from Sássari: *imino rosso*, red intestinal meats including heart and the diaphragm; the rarer *zimino bianco* (white entrails); *fidigheglia a s'ardares*, lambs' intestines with onions, garlic, parsley and white wine vinegar; and *sa cordula*, lambs' entrails roasted or barbecued on a spit or *trippa alla parmigiana* (tripe with parmesan). Snails (*lumache* or *monzette*) also feature on menus.

One of the weirdest delicacies of the island is *casu beccio* or *casu marzu*, a strong, creamy cheese full of live maggots! You won't find it sold commercially and to sample it you will have to ask around and hunt down the farmers who make it. The saying goes that anything that doesn't kill you can feed you.

artichokes and wine *(stufato di capretto)*. Typical main course meats are roast pork, chicken, wild boar and lamb, though the choice varies according to the season. A favourite is *agnello allo spiedo*, spit-roast lamb, best eaten in December. Vegetables come separately and are not a Sardinian strong point. Salads are invariably *verde* (green, that is, lettuce only) or *misto* (mixed, with tomato); artichokes (sometimes served with peas), aubergines and asparagus are usually the best bets.

On the coast, fish fans are spoilt for choice. In many restaurants on or near the sea the menu is 80 percent fish-based. Seafood will include *anguille* (eels), *gamberi* (prawns), *calamari* (squid), *arselle* (clams) and, at the top end of the scale, *aragosta* (lobster), in season from March to the end of August. This is a speciality of Alghero, served Catalan-style, with tomatoes and onions, but it can be found in fish restaurants throughout the island. Cheaper options are *orata* (gilthead bream), *tonno* (tuna), *sogliola* (sole), *spigola* (seabass), *cefalo* (grey mullet) and *pesce spada* (swordfish). Fish is either grilled, lightly fried, baked or served in a marinade or white wine sauce. The smaller fish are served whole at a set price, the larger (for example, swordfish and tuna) will usually be charged by the *etto* (100g). It's quite normal to ask to see the size of a portion first, and check the price. A more acquired taste is *bottarga* or dried mullet roe ('peasant's caviar'), a speciality of Cabras in Oristano where the fish are caught. The eggs are salted, sun-dried between planks, cut into thin slices and served sliced as a starter with extra virgin olive oil or grated over pasta. The island of San Pietro specialises in tuna, caught during the *mattanza (see page 38)* in May and early June. The infinite ways of dishing up the fish, whether fresh, smoked, marinaded, served with oil and lemon or in thin, meat-like slices, will astonish anyone who is only familiar with tuna from the tin.

Bread and Cheese

The crisp, paper-thin *carasau* or *carta da musica*, served in restaurants all over the island, was traditionally made for shepherds when they were away for long periods. *Carasau* comes in various versions: *pane guttiau* is *carasau* dipped in olive oil and salted, served warm; *pane frattau* (also known as *pistoccu*) comes from the Barbagia area and is served with tomato sauce, pecorino cheese and eggs.

The island is well known for its cheeses, and most of Italy's *pecorino* is produced here. Made from ewes' milk it comes in various forms, most commonly the *pecorino romano* and the stronger *pecorino sardo* which is matured for 3–12 months. The sheep's milk from Barbagia is used to make *fiore sardo*, another pecorino, which is matured for several months. *Pecorino* is frequently used in Sardinian cuisine, as is the creamy *ricotta*, also made from ewes' milk.

Cheese and basil

Fruiterer in Santa Teresa di Gallura

Desserts

Sardinians don't excel at desserts despite the abundance of fruit produced on the island. The favourite way to end a meal is with pastries or cakes. Featuring on most menus are *seadas* (or *sebadas*), light pastries filled with ricotta and lemon zest, sprinked with sugar, deep fried and served with Sardinian honey; similar to *seadas* are *pardulas*, filled with ewes' cheese or ricotta, and flavoured with orange and saffron. Lighter options are fresh fruit or *gelati* (ice creams).

Wines

Formerly associated with sweet or fortified wines, Sardinia has made great headway in producing lighter wines to suit contemporary tastes. There are now around 20 wines of DOC status (*Denominazione di Origine Controllata*, indicating a quality wine), most of it coming from cooperatives. Vermentino dominates the dry whites, and notably the amber-coloured, slightly astringent Vermentino di Gallura produced in the hills in the north of the island. This is the only Sardinian wine classified as DOCG (Denominazione di Origine Controllata Garantita), identifying it as a wine from an established wine-producing region maintaining consistently high standards of quality. The best Vermentinos can be sampled at the hilltop wine museum in Berchidda, a wine-producing village of inland Gallusa. Another excellent white which goes well with fish is the dry Torbato, from Alghero; the sparkling version, Torbato Brut, makes a refreshing aperitif.

The best reds are the full-bodied dry Canonnaus, produced mainly around the Gennargentu massif but available throughout the island. The wine is a perfect accompaniment to red meat, game and cheese. The numerous variations of Canonnau include a strong rosé, which goes particularly well with roast suckling pig. Monica wine, a strong dry red produced in the Cágliari district, is similar in flavour to the best red Canonnau, but not as full-bodied. Worth trying too is Carignano del Sulcis, a smooth, full-bodied dry red.

House wine, *vino della casa*, is variable in quality but often perfectly drinkable and very reasonably priced. In the cheaper establishments it will be served in litre or half-litre carafes or jugs. At the other end of the scale, sophisticated restaurants will produce lengthy wine lists featuring international as well as Italian and Sardinian wines.

Dessert Wines and Liqueurs

The most distinctive dessert wine of Sardinia is the Vernaccia di Oristano, produced from vines at the

Wine and water

In restaurants, wine by the glass is almost unheard of, and half bottles can be hard to come by. Bottled water, either still or sparkling, is available in all restaurants, but you can always ask for tap water, which is perfectly safe to drink.

Malvasia from Bosa

mouth of the River Tirso. Amber-coloured and with a hint of bitter almonds, the wine has an alcoholic content of about 15 degrees or more. You may well be offered a complimentary glass before or after a meal – though it's certainly not to everyone's taste. Malvasia from Bosa and Cágliari is similar to Vernaccia and is often served with dessert. The drier sherry-like version is sometimes drunk by locals as a table wine, accompanying fish. Anghelu Ruju from Alghero, a strong, sweet red, makes a fine dessert wine. Another favourite is the sweet white Moscato, either still or sparkling, produced from the Muscat grape which grows in the southwest of the island.

A good meal is usually concluded with a glass of liqueur or a choice of *amari* ('bitters'). At some stage of your stay you are bound to be offered a glass of *mirto*, the ubiquitous herbal liqueur distilled from myrtle which grows all over the island. The superior reddish *mirto rosso* is distilled from the wild myrtle berries, the clear *mirto bianco* from the myrtle leaves. The island's favourite firewater is the grappa-like *filu e ferru* (iron wire) made from grape skins. To conceal evidence of illegal home distillation, farmers used to bury the bottles and use thin iron wires to mark the spot – hence the unusual name.

To Help you Order…

A table for one/ two/three please	**Un tavolo per una persona/ per due/per tre, per favore**
I would like	**Vorrei…**
What would you recommend?	**Cosa ci consiglia?**
How much is it?	**Quanto costa?**
The bill please	**Il conto per favore**

As well as the regional specialities mentioned above, here are some words you are likely to see on Sardinian menus.

acqua	water	**manzo**	beef
aglio	garlic	**melanzane**	aubergine
anguilla	eel	**monzette**	snails
basilico	basil	**ostriche**	oysters
birra	beer	**olio**	oil
burro	butter	**olive**	olives
carciofo	artichoke	**panna**	cream
cinghiale	wild boar	**pane**	bread
cipolle	onions	**patate**	potatoes
coniglio	rabbit	**peperoni**	peppers
fagioli	beans	**pesce**	fish
fagiolini	green beans	**piselli**	peas
finnochio	fennel	**pollo**	chicken
formaggio	cheese	**polpo/pólipo**	octopus
frittata	omelette	**pomodori**	tomatoes
frutti di mare	seafood	**prosciutto**	ham
funghi	mushrooms	**riso**	rice
gamberetti	shrimps	**salsiccia**	sausage
gamberi	prawns	**spinaci**	spinach
gelato	ice cream	**vitello**	veal
insalata	salad	**uova**	eggs
maiale	pork	**zucchini**	courgettes

HANDY TRAVEL TIPS

An A–Z Summary of Practical Information

A

ACCOMMODATION

All hotels are categorised from one to five stars or, at the very top end of the scale, 5-star deluxe. The stars assigned denote facilities and are no indicator of charm or atmosphere. Generally speaking the more stars the higher the price. Tourist offices abroad *(see page 126)* will provide a list of accommodation with addresses, websites and facilities.

In high season you will need to book well in advance. The most crowded times are Easter and late June to early September. In winter many hotels close down; those that remain open offer dramatically cut rates, and this applies in particular to top category hotels. Breakfast is normally included in the room rate. Hotels with their own restaurant will often insist on half board (or occasionally even full board) during the season. Most hotels demand a supplement for a room with a view.

Hotels normally require confirmation of a reservation, which can be done by fax or email. A deposit of one night's stay, payable by credit card, is often requested. Failure to turn up or to inform the hotel in advance of cancellation usually incurs the loss of the deposit.

An appealing alternative to a hotel is an *agriturismo*. Set up by the Italian government in the 1970s to boost the rural economy, these are farm houses which rent out rooms to tourists, often with the option of eating in. Meals are communal affairs, often around the kitchen table and based on home-grown produce. *Agriturismi* have sprouted all over Sardinia, many of them in remote locations well away from the coastal resorts. The properties vary widely – as do the prices – and government controls are very limited. The majority are modern properties, rather than picturesque old farm buildings. Some are equipped with kitchens and rented out on a weekly basis in season. Many establishments organise hiking or horse-riding excursions, or work on the farm. Some sell their own produce such as ham, honey and cheese. It's worth learning at least a few words of Italian since the majority of *agriturismi* owners don't speak English. For details of *agriturismi* try <www.sardinia.net/agritur> or <www.agriturist.it>. With the exception of August, you are unlikely to have problems finding rooms.

The last few years have seen a big rise in the number of B&Bs (Bed and Breakfasts) in a private home, varying from ancient palazzo to modern suburban house. Prices are roughly equivalent to a two-star hotel but in general they offer better value.

I'd like a single/double room	Vorrei una camera singola/ matrimoniale or doppia
with bathroom	con bagno
What's the rate per night?	Quanto si paga per notte?

AIRPORTS

Sardinia is served by three main airports: Elmas at Cágliari, Olbia-Costa Smeralda at Olbia and Fertilia at Alghero. All three handle flights within Italy, as well as charter and scheduled flights from London and other European cities. Airport services include tourist information offices, car rental outlets and banks with ATM machines. Cágliari's airport is 6km (4 miles) from the centre; buses leave at least once an hour and take 15 minutes to Piazza Matteotti in the city centre. Olbia's airport, 5km (3 miles) from the centre, has a bus service every 20 minutes to the city centre taking 10 minutes, and a summer bus service to Arzachena, Palau and Sant Teresa di Gallura to the north. From Fertilia there is a limited bus service to Alghero, 10km (6 miles) away, taking 20 minutes. The Logudoro Tours bus service (tel: 0792 81728) links the airport with Cágliari, via Oristano, connecting with Ryanair flights. Bus services also operate from the airport to Sássari, Santa Teresa di Gallura, Stintino and Nuoro.

B

BUDGETING FOR YOUR TRIP

Generally speaking, prices on the island are average for Italy, but there are wide variations, depending where you stay and at what time of year. In a popular resort such as Santa Teresa di Gallura, hotel prices for the last three weeks in August are double those in spring or autumn. In general the best value accommodation and restaurants tend to be inland from the coast, especially the *agriturismi*. In high season expect to pay €100–150 for a comfortable double with bath or €70–90 in a cheap town hotel. In *agriturismi* you pay from €35 to €60 per person for half board. For a good evening meal in a restaurant expect to pay €30–45, for a light lunch €10–20, coffee or soft drink €1–2, beer in a bar €2–3, spirits €3.50. As in the rest of Italy it's worth bearing in mind that coffee or drinks taken at the bar are far cheaper than those served at a table on the terrace. Car hire is quite pricey at €250–300 a week for a small car and petrol prices are high.

Entry fees to museums and archaeological sites vary from €1 to €6; entrance is free for EU citizens under 18 and over 65.

C

CAMPING

Sardinia has around 90 designated sites, mainly around the coast. Some of these are huge complexes complete with pools, restaurants, shops and sports facilities. Accommodation can be in caravans or bungalows as well as ready-erected tents. Details of campsites can be found at <www.campeggi.com> or at <www.camping.it>.

Is there a campsite near here?   C'è un campeggio qui vicino?
We have a tent/caravan (trailer).   Abbiamo la tenda/la roulotte.

Alternatively, local tourist offices can supply lists for their area. Campsites are normally open from Easter to October. Camping rough is forbidden.

CAR HIRE

Although much of the island can be covered by bus or train, services tend to be slow and infrequent; to really explore the island you need to hire a car. Bookings made and paid for in advance of travel can work out cheaper than hiring a car once you are in Sardinia. Be sure to read the terms and conditions carefully before you go – local suppliers have a habit of making you pay for extras you may not need.

Cars can be picked up at the main airports, where the major car-hire companies have their outlets. Drivers must present their own national driving licence or one that is internationally recognised. There is a small additional charge for an extra driver. Credit card imprints are taken as a deposit and are normally the only form of payment acceptable. 'Inclusive' prices do not normally include personal accident insurance, windscreens, tyres and wheels. Make sure you return the car with a full tank of fuel – there are hefty refuelling charges if you fail to do so.

I would like to hire a car	**Vorrei noleggiare una macchina**
for one day	**per un giorno**
for one week	**per una settimana**

CLIMATE

Sardinia's climate is typical of the Mediterranean, with long. hot summers, warm springs and autumns and mild winters. A good time to go is May when it's usually warm and sunny, the beaches are uncrowded and the countryside is strewn with wild flowers. Autumn is pleasant too, and the waters are still warm enough for swimming in late September or even October. The really hot months are July and August when temperatures soar to 30°C (86°F) or more. But sea breezes bring welcome relief from the heat. Less pleasant are the *maestrale* and *ponente* winds (from the northwest and west respectively). In winter the average coastal temperatures are 10–14°C (50–57°F); the interior, however, is far colder and snow sometimes covers the highest peaks. Rain falls mainly in winter and autumn, with a few sudden showers during the spring. Here the average temperatures for Cagliari:

	J	F	M	A	M	J	J	A	S	O	N	D
Max °F	57	59	63	66	73	81	86	86	81	73	66	61
°C	14	15	17	19	23	27	30	30	27	23	19	16
Min °F	47	51	48	51	57	64	70	70	66	59	51	48
°C	7	11	9	11	14	18	21	21	19	15	11	9

CLOTHING

As in most Catholic countries, the wearing of miniskirts, skimpy shorts or shoulderless garments in churches is likely to cause offence. Sauntering around streets in scanty clothing or swimwear may also offend locals, especially in towns inland. Only the very smartest restaurants and those in the top hotels require jacket-and-tie formality. Casual clothes are quite acceptable in most trattorias.

CRIME AND SAFETY

The crime rate in Sardinia is low and visitors can stroll through the streets without any threat. There are, however, occasional instances of petty theft and it's wise to take simple precautions: always lock car doors and never leave valuables visible inside; leave important documents and valuables in the hotel safe; wear a money bag or if carrying a shoulder bag, make sure it faces away from the street to deter motorcyclists who can snatch bags at high speed.

| I want to report a theft | **Voglio denunciare un furto** |
| My wallet/passport/ticket has been stolen | **Mi hanno rubato il portafoglio/ il passaporto/il biglietto** |

CUSTOMS AND ENTRY REQUIREMENTS

For citizens of EU countries, a valid passport or identity card is all that is needed to enter Italy for stays of up to 90 days. Citizens of Australia, Canada, New Zealand and the US require a valid passport.

Visas *(permesso di soggiorno)*. For stays of more than 90 days a visa or residence permit is needed. Contact your country's Italian embassy.

Customs. Free exchange of non-duty-free goods for personal use is allowed between EU countries. Refer to your home country's regulating organisation for a current complete list of import restrictions.

Currency restrictions. Tourists may bring an unlimited amount of Italian or foreign currency into the country. On departure you must declare any currency beyond the equivalent of €12,500, so it's wise to declare sums exceeding this amount when you arrive.

| I have nothing to declare. | **Non ho nulla da dichiarare.** |
| It's for my personal use. | **È per mio uso personale.** |

D

DRIVING

Entering Italy

To bring your car into Italy, you will need:

- an international driving licence or valid national one
- car registration papers
- green insurance card (an extension to your ordinary insurance, making your policy valid for Italy – not a legal requirement but strongly recommended)

- a red warning triangle in case of breakdown
- national identity sticker for your car
- visibility vest (in case of breakdown).

patente	driving licence
libretto di circolazione	car registration papers
carta verde	green card

The main highways linking the cities are fast and surprisingly empty. There are no motorways (and hence no tolls), and the main roads are mostly dual carriageway. The SS131 (the Carlo Felice highway) links Cágliari in the south with Sássari and Porto Torres in the north, with a branch linking Abbastanta and Olbia, via Nuoro. In remote areas, such as the Gennargentu mountains, roads are not so good and sign-posting is random. Detours to beaches along seemingly never-ending dirt tracks can be long and tiring, especially (as in the Costa Smeralda) when they come to a halt at some smart villa complex with no public access to the beach. Many of the most scenic routes on the island are tortuous coastal or mountain roads where you need to watch out for reckless local drivers overtaking on blind bends.

| Are we on the right road for..? | Siamo sulla strada giusta per...? |

Rules of the Road
Drive on the right, pass on the left. Speed limits are 50km/h (30mph) in towns and built-up areas, 90km/h (55mph) on normal roads and 110km/h (70mph) on main highways. At roundabouts the traffic from the right has the right of way. Seat belts are compulsory in the front and back, and children should be properly restrained. The blood alcohol limit is 0.05 percent (stricter than the UK which is

0.08 percent) and random breath tests do occur. Since 2002 it has been compulsory for all drivers on Italian highways to keep dipped headlights switched on (day as well as night) – though many drivers ignore the regulation.

Breakdowns

In case of accident or breakdown call 113 (General Emergencies) or the Automobile Club of Italy on 803 116. The club has an efficient 24-hour service which is available to foreign visitors.

I've had a breakdown.	**Ho avuto un guasto.**
There's been an accident.	**C'è stato un incidente.**

Petrol

Many petrol stations close between 12.30 and 3.30pm, but there are plenty of '24-hour' stations with self-service dispensers accepting euro notes and credit cards. The main highways have regularly spaced filling stations, but in remote inland regions they are predictably sparse. The majority but certainly not all petrol stations accept credit cards.

Fill it up please.	**Faccia il pieno per favore.**

Parking

Finding a parking space in cities and main towns can be a nightmare – even off-season. If you are lucky enough to find a space, you may need to purchase a special 'scratchcard', only available from

Where's the nearest car park?	**Dov'è il parcheggio più vicino?**
Can I park here?	**Posso parcheggiare qui?**

tobaccanists and bars. The card has to be displayed in the car, with details of the date and time of parking. Other street parking is controlled by meters or parking attendants.

E

ELECTRICITY

The electrical current is 220V, AC; sockets take two-pin, round-pronged plugs. Visitors from the UK will require an adaptor.

EMBASSIES

If you lose your passport or need other help, contact your nearest national embassy or consulate.

Australia: Via Antonio Bosio 5, 00161 Rome, tel: 06-852721, <www.italy.embassy.gov.au>.

Canada: Via Zara 30, 00198 Rome, tel: 06-85441, <www.rome. gc.ca>.

Ireland: Piazza Campitelli 3, 00186 Rome, tel: 06-6979121.

New Zealand: Via Zara 28, 00198 Rome, tel: 06-4417171, <www.nzembassy.com>.

UK: Via XX Settembre 80a, 00187 Rome, tel: 06-42200001, <www.britishembassy.gov.uk>.

US: Via Vittorio Veneto 121, 00187 Rome, tel: 06-46741, <www. usembassy.it>.

EMERGENCIES

General emergencies:	113	Fire:	115
Police:	112	Ambulance:	118

Careful!	**Attenzione!**
Help!	**Aiuto!**
Stop thief!	**Al ladro!**

G

GAY AND LESBIAN TRAVELLERS

Sardinia is conservative compared with the cosmoplitan cities of northern Italy. Although not necessarily averse to gay couples travelling together, locals do not always tolerate overt displays of affection. There are a few gay bars and clubs, notably in the cities and larger resorts, but no real gay scene. To find general information and listings of gay venues within Italy, contact ArciGay, the national gay rights organisation, at Via Don Minzoni 18, Bologna, tel: 051-649 3055, <www.arcigay.it>.

GETTING TO SARDINIA

By Air

An increasing number of low-cost airlines now fly direct to Sardinia from the UK and other European destinations. The no-frills Ryanair (<www.ryanair.com>) flies from Stansted, Coventry, East Midlands and Dublin to Alghero. Even in August the mid-week flights are very reasonably priced if you book well in advance, and off-season can be little more than the cost of the airport tax. EasyJet (<www.easyjet.com>) flies from Luton to Cágliari and from Gatwick to Olbia. Thomsonfly (<www.thomsonfly.com>) operate services to Olbia from Gatwick and Manchester airports. Scheduled airlines have been forced to cut the costs of flights to compete with low-cost airlines. British Airways (<www.ba.com>) flies direct to Cágliari from Gatwick, and Meridiana (<www.meridiana.it>) to Olbia from Gatwick.

There are currently no direct flights from long-haul destinations. Passengers from the US, Canada, New Zealand and Australia can fly to Rome or Milan and take one of the many connecting flights to Sardinia; but before booking, it's worth comparing the cost of a cheap flight to London, and then a charter or flight with a low-cost airline to Sardinia.

By Ferry

Sardinia is well connected to Italian mainland ports. Ferry services operate to the island from Civitavecchia, Fiumicino, Naples, Livorno, La Spezia and Genoa; also from Palermo and Trapani in Sicily, and from Tunis in Tunisia. The main ferry companies operating services to the mainland are Tirrenia (<www.tirrenia.it>) and Moby (<www.moby.it>). The shortest route between mainland Italy and Sardinia is Civitavecchia to Olbia, which takes 4–7 hours depending on the type of ferry. Prices vary accordingly. Many services operate from Easter to October only and some of the faster services are restricted to high season only. Sardinia also has ferry links with France, connecting Marseilles with Porto Torres in the north (14–17 hours) from April to October, and a regular all-year service between Bonifacio in Corsica and the resort of Santa Teresa di Gallura.

GUIDES AND TOURS

Local tourist offices, travel agencies and hotels can provide details of guides and tours. Guides are particularly useful for archaeological sites – where the stone towers or mounds of rubble mean little to the untrained eye – and are certainly advisable for tackling the highest peaks of the Gennargentu massif and other regions of the interior.

Sardinian Way (<www.sardinianway.it>), which promotes sustainable tourism, operates various walking, biking and jeep tours. The emphasis is placed on nature, the environment, archaeology and local gastronomy.

H

HEALTH AND MEDICAL CARE

All EU countries have reciprocal arrangements for reclaiming the costs of medical services. UK residents should obtain the European

Health Insurance Card, available from post offices or online. This only covers you for medical care, not for emergency repatriation costs or additional expenses such as accommodation and flights for anyone travelling with you. To cover all eventualities a travel insurance policy is advisable, and for non-EU residents, essential. For insurance claims, make sure you keep all receipts for medical treatment and any medicines prescribed. Vaccinations are not needed for Italy, but take with you sunscreen and mosquito repellent in the summer. Tap water is safe to drink in Sardinia, unless you see the sign *Acqua non potabile*. However, many visitors prefer to copy the locals and drink mineral water.

A pharmacy *(farmacia)* is identified by a green cross. All main towns offer a 24-hour pharmacy service, with a night-time and Sunday rota. After-hours locations are listed in local papers and posted on all pharmacy doors. Italian pharmacists are well trained to deal with minor ailments and although they do not stock quantities of foreign medicines can usually supply the local equivalent. If you need a doctor *(medico)* ask at the pharmacy, your hotel or consult the yellow pages. For serious cases or emergencies, dial 118 for an ambulance or head for the *Pronto Soccorso* (Accident and Emergency) of the local hospital. This will also deal with emergency dental treatment.

I need a doctor/a dentist.	**Ho bisogno di un medico/ dentista.**
Where's the nearest (all-night) chemist?	**Dov'è la farmacia (di turno) più vicina?**

HOLIDAYS

Most shops shut on national public holidays. As well as the main holidays listed below, some towns also take a public holiday to celebrate the local saint's day.

1 January	New Year's Day
6 January	Epiphany
March/April	Easter
March/April	Easter Monday
25 April	Liberation Day
1 May	Labour Day
15 August	Ferragosto; Assumption Day
1 November	All Saints' Day
8 December	Feast of the Immaculate Conception
25 December	Christmas
26 December	St Stephen's Day

L

LANGUAGE

Sardinia has two languages – standard Italian and *Sardo* or Sardinian. The island tongue reflects a host of different influences; the roots are in Latin, but the language was later modified by the various European powers who invaded the island, notably the Spanish. In Alghero an old version of Spanish Catalan can still be heard in the streets; on the island of Sant'Antioco a Ligurian dialect is still spoken. Each region has its own dialect, and some Sards can only communicate with each other by conversing in Italian. This is particularly true of inland Sardinia, while on the coasts there is more emphasis on Italian than on Sardinian dialects.

Sardinians do not have the command of English that you find in, say, Rome or Florence. The vast majority of tourists here are Italian, and although you will find English speakers in the main resorts and towns, elsewhere locals are only likely to speak a smattering of English, if that. Sardinians are appreciative of visitors who speak some Italian and (unlike Florentines and Venetians) don't have the infuriating habit of replying in broken English when you speak to them in Italian.

M

MAPS

Sardinia is such a large island that even the best maps don't mark every little road. For exploring the island the best road maps are the Touring Club Italiano at 1:200,000 and the Automobile Club d'Italia at 1:275,000. Maps are available at bookstores and kiosks thoughout the island, but the better ones are more readily available in specialist map or travel book shops abroad.

MEDIA

Newspapers. English and and foreign newspapers are available, at least a day late, in the cities and main resorts during the season. A good substitute is the *International Herald Tribune* available in the main centres from Monday to Saturday. The two main island newspapers are Cágliari's *L'Unione Sarda* and Sássari's *La Nuova Sardegna* (known as '*La Nuova*').

Have you any English-language **Avete giornali in inglese?**
newspapers?

Television. Many hotels provide satellite TV, though you won't necessarily be able to gain access to English-language channels. As regards Italian TV, there are the state-run RAI 1, 2 and 3, plus numerous private channels pouring out tacky soaps, films and non-stop ads. The state-run radio stations, RAI 1, 2 and 3, mainly broadcast news bulletins and music.

MONEY

The unit of currency in Italy is the euro (€) divided into 100 cents. Euro notes come in denominations of 500, 200, 100, 50, 20, 10 and 5; coins in denominations of 2 and 1; then 50, 20, 10, 5, 2 and 1 cents.

Exchange Facilities. Banks and post offices tend to offer the best rates, followed by bureaux de change and hotels. Some bureaux de change offer commission-free facilities, but the rate of exchange is usually higher than that of the banks. Traveller's cheques can be exchanged on presentation of a passport, but tend to attract a high commission and sometimes a transaction fee on top. Note too that not all hotels or shops in Sardinia will accept traveller's cheques.

Credit Cards and ATMs. The major credit cards are accepted in most hotels and restaurants, petrol stations, stores and supermarkets. Some of the smaller hotels, *agriturismi* and B&Bs will only accept cash, and the same is true of simple trattorias. For withdrawals of cash, ATM machines (or Bancomats) can be found all over the island.

I want to change some pounds/dollars.	Desidero cambiare delle sterline/dei dollari.
Do you accept traveller's cheques?	Accetta i traveller's cheques?
Can I pay with a credit card?	Posso pagare con la carta di credito?

OPENING HOURS

Major museums, archaeological sites and caves are open all day every day. Others vary widely, but most are closed for lunch, from 12.30 or 1pm to 3.30–4.30pm and for one day a week, normally Monday. Archaeological sites often remain open until an hour before sunset. Most churches are open daily from 7 or 8am to 12 or 12.30pm, and from 4 or 5pm to 7 or 8pm. In general banks open Monday to Friday 8.30am–1 or 1.30pm and some also open for an hour or so in the afternoon from 2.30 or 3pm to 4 or 5pm. Some banks also open on

Saturday mornings. Shops are open Monday–Saturday 8 or 9am to 1pm, and 4 or 5pm to 7 or 8pm, though some supermarkets and main town stores are open all day. In summer, tourist shops in main resorts such as Alghero are open until 10pm.

P

POLICE

The *Polizia Urbana*, or city police, regulate traffic and enforce local laws, while the *Carabinieri* are the armed military police who handle public law and order. The *Politizia Stradale* patrol the highways and other roads. In an emergency the Carabinieri can be reached on 112 – or you can ring the general emergency number, 113.

| Where's the nearest police station? | Dov'è il posto di polizia più vicino? |

POST OFFICES

Main branches are open Monday to Friday 8.30am–6.30 or 7.30pm, Saturday 8.30am–12.30 or 1pm, sub post offices Monday to Friday 8.30am–2pm, Saturday 8.30am–noon. The postal service is slow, and for important communications it is best to use the more expensive express system. Main post offices offer a poste restante service. Correspondence should be addressed to Fermo Posta, Ufficio Postale Principale, followed by the name of the town where you wish to pick it up. You will need some form of identification on collection. Stamps *(francobolli)* can be bought from tobacconists, as well as from post offices.

| I'd like a stamp for this letter/postcard. | Desidero un francobollo per questa lettera/cartolina. |

PUBLIC TRANSPORT

Bus. The bus network covers virtually the whole island, including some of the tiniest villages in the mountainous interior. But services are sparse and the journeys very time-consuming. The fast services operate between the main towns: Cágliari, Oristano, Sássari, Nuoro and Olbia – for example, Cágliari to Sássari takes three hours non-stop, or four with stops en route. Certain services, particularly those to beaches or other tourist attractions, operate only in the summer months. The main bus company is the Azienda Regionale Sarda Trasporti (ARST; <www.arst.sardegna.it> in Italian only). From June to September tourist passes are available on their buses for one, two, three or four weeks. The large towns have good bus systems and the service is cheap. Tickets should be bought in advance at bars, tobacconists or newspaper stands and then stamped once you board the bus.

Trains. Services are provided both by the state-run Ferrovie dello Stato (FS; <www.ferroviedellostato.it>) and the private Ferrovie della Sardegna (<www.ferroviesardegna.it>). Trains tend to be slow and services infrequent. Trenitalia provides a service linking main towns – for example, Cágliari to Sássari (4 hrs), Cágliari to Olbia (4 hrs) and Sássari to Oristano (2½ hrs); FdS provides some of the local services and also runs the delightful *Trenino Verde*. The narrow-gauge 'Little Green Train' chugs its way through some of the most remote and beautiful regions of the island. Provided you don't mind nearly five hours in uncomfortable vintage carriages, and returning (if needs be) the next day, try out the route from Mandas, 69km (43 miles) from Cágliari, all the way to the port of Arbatax on the east coast. The service was set up in 1888; today it runs during summer months only and is primarily for tourists. The service also covers the Nuoro–Bosa route and several lines in the Sássari region. One of the most popular routes is Sássari–Tempio Pausania–Palau, through oaks and granite masses to Tempio Pausania, then descending to the north coast with beautiful views over the Arcipelago della Maddalena.

Ferries. Regular car-ferry services connect Palau in the north of the island with the island of La Maddalena, and Portovesme in the southwest with the Isola di San Pietro.

When is the next ferry/ train/bus to…?	**Quando parte il prossimo traghetto/autobus/treno per…?**
Where can I buy a ticket?	**Dove posso comparare un biglietto?**
One way/roundtrip	**Andata/andata e ritorno**

R

RELIGION

Like the rest of Italy, Sardinia is primarily Roman Catholic. The church plays a major role in the community and, while numbers of churchgoers have fallen in recent years, the majority of Sardinians are still regular worshippers.

T

TELEPHONE

Calls can be made from public telephones with a prepaid phone card (*scheda telefónica*), available from *tabacchi* or newspaper stands. Remember to rip off the perforated corner before calling. Payphones have instructions in English for international and other calls. Post offices and tobacconists sell international telephone cards (€5 and €10) with a pin number which can be used from public telephones, land lines and mobiles. Instructions are given in English on the card. When phoning abroad, dial 00 for the international code, followed by the city or area code and then the number. Calls can also be made with a charge card bought from your telephone company prior to travel. This is useful for telephoning from hotels, which levy hefty surcharges on long-distance calls. The cheapest time to telephone from Italy is 10pm to 8am on weekdays and all day Sunday. Italian area codes have now all been incorporated into the numbers, so even if you are calling from the same town you are telephoning, the code needs to be included.

Mobile Phones. In 2007 the European Commission introduced strict caps on roaming charges, cutting costs for some users by over 50 percent. The rates, which are to be reduced further in 2008, do not apply to text messaging. If your mobile cannot receive or make calls in Italy (check with your mobile company before leaving) you can purchase an SIM 'pay as you go' card *(scheda pre-pagata)* in any mobile phone shop and have a new mobile number for the length of your stay.

Give me … coins/phone **Per favore, mi dia**
card please. **una scheda telefonica.**
5 euros/25 euros **cinque euro/venticinque euro**

TIME ZONES

Like the rest of Italy, Sardinia is one hour ahead of Greenwich Mean Time (GMT).

New York	Sardinia	Jo'burg	Sydney	Auckland
7am	noon	1pm	9pm	11pm

TIPPING

A 10–15 percent service charge is often included in restaurant bills, and although a tip will be appreciated, no extra is expected. For quick service in bars, leave a coin or two with your till receipt when ordering. Taxi drivers do not expect a tip but it is normal to round up the fare.

TOILETS

Public ones are hard to find, but you can always use toilets in cafés and bars. Buying a drink at the same time will be appreciated.

TOURIST INFORMATION

Within Sardinia you will find a tourist office (Azienda Autonoma di Soggiorno e Turismo, or AAST) in most towns and main resorts. The majority are helpful and can supply you with maps, pamphlets and details of accommodation and local attractions. However, some of the staff in the smaller offices have a very limited command of English. Centres with no official tourist office may have a *Pro Loco* in the town hall which serves a similar purpose but is open for limited hours in summer only. Failing that you can always try the local tour agencies, who organise excursions and car hire, and can provide general information. Most tourist offices are open Monday to Friday 9am–1pm and 4–7pm, Saturday 9am–1pm, though some of the minor offices keep shorter hours. The Alghero office is the best equipped on the island, and from April to October is open from Monday to Saturday 8am–8pm, November to March 8am–2pm.

To obtain information on Sardinia prior to travel, contact the Italian National Tourist Office (ENIT) in your home country.

Where's the tourist office?   **Dov'è l'ufficio turistico?**

Italian Tourist Offices Abroad
Canada: Suite 907, South Tower, 175 Bloor Street East, Toronto, Ontario ON M4W3R8, tel: 416-925 4882
UK: 1 Princes Street, London W1B 2AY, tel: 020-7408 1254, <www.enit.it>.
USA: 630 Fifth Avenue, Suite 1565, New York, NY 10111, tel: 212-245 5618

500 North Michigan Ave, Suite 2240, Chicago, Illinois 60611, tel: 312-644 0996
12400 Wilshire Blvd, Suite 550, Los Angeles, CA 90025, tel: 310-820 1898
The website for North America and Canada is <www.italian tourism.com>.

Main Tourist Offices in Sardinia
Alghero: Piazza Porta Terra 9, tel: 0799 79054.
Cágliari: Piazza Matteotti 9, tel: 0706 69255; also at Stazione Marittima, tel: 0706 68352. ESIT, the Sardinian Tourist Information Office, covering the whole of Sardinia, but not very useful, is at Via Mameli 97, Cágliari, tel: 0706 0231.
Olbia: Via Castello Piro, tel: 0789 21453.

W

WEBSITES AND INTERNET CAFÉS

The official tourist site is **www.sardegnaturismo.it**. Also try:
www.sardinia.net useful general site
www.sardiniapoint.it useful general site in Italian
www.getaroundsardinia.com itineraries and public transport
Internet cafés and points can be found in the main towns and resorts. For a list, go to: **http://cafe.ecs.net/sardegna.htm**.

Y

YOUTH HOSTELS

The island has official youth hostels in four locations: Alghero, Bosa, Castelsardo and Muravera. An HI (Hostelling International) card is required, but temporary membership is available. For information and reservations (which are essential in summer), log on to <www.ostellionline.org>.

Recommended Hotels

Tourism on the island didn't really take off until the 1960s and the typical Sardinian hotel is a modern, sea-view building, strong on facilities but short on charm and character. Those listed below stand out, either for setting, ambiance, food, good value – or if you are lucky, all four. At the top end of the market are the exclusive hotels of the Costa Smeralda, which fetch some of the highest prices in Italy, and those of Santa Margherita di Pula, south of Cágliari. At the other end of the scale are the increasingly popular B&Bs (Bed and Breakfasts) and the now abundant *agriturismi (see page 107)* where you can stay on a farm or rural property and see the local way of life.

   The symbols below are a rough indication of what you can expect to pay for a twin room with bathroom, including breakfast, in high season. Many hotels insist on half board, especially in summer.

€€€€	over 210 euros
€€€	150–210 euros
€€	100–150 euros
€	below 100 euros

ALGHERO AND THE NORTHWEST

ALGHERO

Porto Conte €€€ *Località Porto Conte, 07041 Alghero, tel: 0799 42035, fax: 0799 42045, <www.hotelportoconte.com>.* Large but low-rise, Catalan-style hotel amid pines and palms right on the bay of Porto Conte. The pool and garden area lead on to a sandy beach, equipped with facilities (at extra cost) and beach club. Guest rooms look out on to the gardens or, ideally, across the clear blue waters of the bay.

San Francesco € *Via Ambrogio Machin 2, tel/fax: 0799 80330, <www.sanfrancescohotel.com>.* A rather special place in that it's the only hotel in the old town, and the rooms focus on the lovely cloister of the Church of San Franceso. (The building used to be the convent for the church.) The only public area apart from Reception is a basic breakfast room/bar off the cloister. The 20 bedrooms are nothing special, but they are clean and come with private bathroom.

Villa Las Tronas €€€€ *Lungomare Valencia 1, 07041 Alghero, tel: 0799 81818, fax: 0799 81044, <www.hvlt.com>.* You can't miss this castellated building set on a private rocky promontory just south of Alghero. It was built at the end of the 19th century and in the 1940s it was home to the Italian royal family during their holidays in Sardinia. For many years it has been a small, exclusive and elegant hotel. Guest rooms have sea views, art nouveau furnishings and modern bathrooms. There is no beach, but you can swim in the seawater pool or from the rocky terraces around it.

BOSA

La Corte Fiorita €–€€ *Via Lungo Temo de Gaspari, tel: 0785 377058, <www.albergo-diffuso.it>.* Three of central Bosa's medieval buildings have been beautifully restored to form this rustic-style hotel. The main building ('Le Palme'), complete with breakfast room, patio and reading room, is a narrow 4-storey house overlooking the River Temo; the annexes ('I Gerani' and 'Le Concc') are on narrow alleys nearby. All rooms have large bathrooms and some have balconies.

Sa Pischedda € *Via Roma 8, 08013 Bosa, tel: 0785 373065, fax: 0785 370177, <www.hotelsapischedda.it>.* Built in 1895 this was one of the first three hotels on the island. It has frescoes in reception and marble-topped antiques in public areas. Bedrooms are modern, smallish and sparsely furnished, some with capacity for four guests. The restaurant is well worth trying for local lobster, fish soup or prawns, cooked in the local Malvasia wine.

STINTINO

Silvestrino €€ *Via Sassari, 14, 07040 Stintino, tel: 0795 23007, fax: 0795 23473, <www.silvestrino.it>.* A small, family-run hotel with a first-rate fish restaurant *(see page 137)*, spotless guest rooms and a welcoming atmosphere. Located in the centre of the fishing village, it has 11 rooms varying in size, comfort and price (the most desirable room is No. 25 at the top with its own solarium). Prices virtually double in summer – the village and the nearby Pelosa beach are hugely popular with tourists in season.

ARZACHENA

Ca' La Somara €–€€ *Loc. Sarra Balestra, 07020 Arzachena, tel: 0789 98969, <www.italiaagriturismo.net/calasomara>.* As the crow flies the Ca' La Somara (House of the Donkey) is only 4km (2½ miles) from the Costa Smeralda; yet it couldn't be more different from the luxury hotels along the coast. A peaceful *agriturismo*, it was converted from sheep stables to provide a welcoming, relaxing and rural retreat. Donkeys graze nearby and the farmhouse retains its rustic features. Meals, using vegetables from the farm, are served on request. Walking and riding excursions can be arranged.

Cala di Volpe €€€€ *Costa Smeralda, 07020 Porto Cervo, tel: 0789 976111, <www.starwoodhotels.com>.* Exclusive and outrageously expensive hotel on the Costa Smeralda. One of the first tourist hotels on the island, it was built in rustic style with arches, beams and rough-plastered walls. Facilities include a fabulous seawater pool, tennis, watersports, shops and a private launch to the beach.

Capriccioli €€€ *Loc. Capriccioli, Costa Smeralda, tel: 0789 96004, fax: 0789 96422, <www.hotelcapriccioli.it>.* One of the less exorbitant hotels on the Costa Smeralda. It started life as a tiny family-run restaurant – the first on the Costa Smeralda. Now it's a 45-bedroom 4-star hotel with a large sea-view restaurant, swimming pool and tennis court. Bedrooms can be a bit cramped but are well equipped. Half board is compulsory. Steps lead down to a pretty – and very popular – little beach.

Lu Pastruccialeddu € *P.O. Box 39, 07021 Arzachena, tel: 0789 81777, <www.pastruccialeddu.com>.* This stone B&B has a peaceful setting with 50 hectares (124 acres) of private land, but is only

5km (3 miles) from the lovely beaches of the Costa Smeralda. The three guest rooms have TV and private bathrooms. Breakfasts of delicious home-made pastries and jams are served in a rustic dining room. Minimum stay is two nights or one week in July and August.

SANTA TERESA DI GALLURA

Bellavista € *Via Sonnino 8, 07028 Santa Teresa di Gallura, tel/fax: 0789 754162.* The hotel hotel lives up to its name – at least from six of the rooms and the restaurant. A pink block with green shutters, it perches above Santa Teresa's main Rena Bianca beach. Bedrooms are somewhat basic but this is a good option if you're economising. Half board is compulsory in season – but the menu changes every day.

Corallaro €€€ *Località Rena Bianca, 07028 Santa Teresa di Gallura, tel: 0789 755475, fax: 0789 755431, <www.hotelcorallaro.it>.* Santa Teresa's best-known hotel, set back from the Rena Bianca beach in the centre. Surprisingly few rooms have sea views (you pay a hefty daily supplement for the privilege) but it's pleasantly light and airy throughout. Facilities include spacious public rooms, gym, outdoor pool and indoor pool which opens off-season 'at the management's discretion'.

Moresco €€ *Via Imbriani 16, 07028 Sant Teresa di Gallura, tel: 0789 754118, fax: 0789 755085, <www.morescohotel.it>.* A cheaper alternative to the Corallaro, the pink-arcaded Moresco is set 100m/yds up from the Rena Bianca beach. Over half the rooms look out across the Straits of Bonifacio, with views of Corsica on a clear day. Half board is compulsory, but the food is good, and it's served in a sea-view restaurant, with terrace. The beach is packed in season, but the section nearest the Moresco is reserved for guests.

NUORO AND THE EAST

ÁRBATAX

Relais Monte Turri €€€–€€€€ *Località Monte Turri, 08041 Árbatax, tel: 0782 667500, fax: 0782 667892, <www.mobygest.it>.*

Romantic retreat perched above the coast with stunning sea views. Accommodation is divided between the main Torre (Tower) and stone-built cottages in the gardens 40m (130ft) below. A lift takes you down to a small man-made beach within a rocky cove. The Torre has an outdoor pool, small gym, beauty centre, sauna and restaurant with inviting open-air terrace.

DORGALI

L'Oasi €€ *Via García Lorca 13, 08022 Cala Gonone, tel: 0784 93111, fax: 0784 93444, <www.loasihotel.it>.* Family-run hotel occupying a wonderful spot high above the port, with sweeping views of the sea and coast. The buildings are set among gardens and pines, with terraces and balconies making the most of the views. A short cut takes you down to the port where there's a wide choice of boat excursions along the coast. Stays are normally for a minimum of three days, or seven in August.

OLIENA

Su Gologone €€€ *Loc. Su Gologone, 08025 Oliena, tel: 0784 287512, fax: 0784 287668, <www.sugologone.it>.* Inland Sardinia's most famous hotel and restaurant, beautifully located among olive trees and pinewoods below the Supramonte mountains. The restaurant *(see pages 58 and 139)* is renowned for suckling pig, which sizzles at the huge fireplace in the dining room. Guest rooms are all prettily furnished with hand-embroidered local fabrics, and walls throughout are hung with artworks by island artists. Facilities include a large swimming pool, fitness centre and tennis courts. Landrover safaris into the Barbagia, horse-riding and trekking are regularly organised.

ORISTANO AND THE WEST

ORISTANO

Eleonora € *Piazza Eleonora 12, 09170 Oristano, tel/fax: 0783 70435, <www.eleonora-bed-and-breakfast.com>.* This delightful

B&B occupies two floors of an old *palazzo* overlooking the handsome 19th-century Piazza Eleonara in the heart of the old town. The large rooms retain original features and some antiques. Breakfasts are served in the garden in summer. No credit cards.

PISCINAS

Le Dune €€€–€€€€ *Via Bau, 1 Fra. Ingurtosu, 09031 Arbus, tel: 0709 77130, fax: 0709 77230, <www.leduneingurtosu.it>*. Stylish conversion of an old mining building on the glorious beach of Piscinas, accessed along a 7km (4½-mile) dirt track from Ingurtosu. The 25 guest rooms have bamboo and rattan furnishings, and all mod cons. Half- or full-board is compulsory.

CÁGLIARI AND THE SOUTHEAST

CÁGLIARI

AeR Bundes Jack Vittoria € *Via Roma 75, 09124 Cágliari, tel: 0706 67970, fax: 0706 67970, email: <hotel.aerbundesjack@libero.it>*. Friendly, family-run hotel on the third floor of a 1920s building overlooking the ferry port. Original features such as stucco ceilings have been preserved and bedrooms have good, solid furniture. Breakfast (which is extra) is served only in summer, but there are plenty of inviting cafés under the arcades of Via Roma.

T Hotel €€–€€€€ *Via dei Giudicati, tel: 0704 74001, <www.thotel.it>*. Cagliari's first designer hotel opened in 2005. Modern and stylish, it incorporates a 15-storey steel-and-glass round tower, whose upper floors have panoramic views. Guest rooms come with king-size beds, Ikea-style furnishing, along with vibrant shades of either orange or red – or the more tranquil green or blue. Amenities include a minimalist bar and garden-view bistro, which are popular rendezvous for the Cagliaresi, and a wellness centre. Although more geared to business travellers than tourists (the hotel is about 2km/1 mile) from the historic centre with few restaurants nearby), you can get rooms at bargain prices in summer when business trade declines.

SANTA MARGHERITA DI PULA

Forte Village Resort €€€€ *09010 Santa Margherita di Pula, tel: 0709 2171, fax: 0709 21246, <www.fortevillageresort.com>*. Vast luxury complex set in 22 hectares (55 acres) of gardens by the beach. The resort comprises seven hotels, all five- and four-star, 10 swimming pools, 21 restaurants, wellness centre and numerous watersports. Excellent children's facilities include a miniclub, crèche and babysitting.

MarePineta €€ *09010 Santa Margherita di Pula, tel: 0709 208361, fax: 0709 208359, <www.hotelflamingo.it>*. The cheaper sister of the nearby Hotel Flamingo, inconspicuously located among the beachside pines. Accommodation is in attractively furnished individual bungalows behind the hotel, while public rooms focus on the sea and the white sandy beach. Guests have the use of the Flamingo facilities. Half board only.

SAN VITO

I Glicini € *Via Nazionale 187, 09040 San Vito, tel: 0709 929042, <www.bedandbreakfastiglicini.com>*. There is no reason to visit the town of San Vito other than to stay at this splendid town mansion. The oldest part dates from 1800 and the house has been in the same family for four generations. From the main street a huge wooden portal opens on to a delightful courtyard where breakfasts are taken at a communal table. Guest rooms with wood floors, pine furnishings and good bathrooms have been converted at the back of the house.

THE SOUTHWEST

ISOLA DI SAN PIETRO

Hieracon €€ *Corso Cavour, 62, 09014 Carloforte, tel: 0781 854028, fax: 0781 854893, <www.hotelhieracon.com>*. Art nouveau hotel with an elegant pale façade overlooking the port. Guest rooms in the main building, apartments in the garden, all with TV and air conditioning. Breakfast in summer is taken in the shade of palm trees, other meals in the main restaurant with sea-view terrace tables.

Recommended Restaurants

The restaurants recommended below range from smart dining establishments to family-run pizzerias and cafés. Normal opening times are lunch *(pranzo)*, 12.30–3pm, and the evening meal *(cena)*, 8–10pm or even later in main resorts. Lunch is traditionally the main meal of the day and some rural trattorias close in the evening. Pizzerias are numerous; the best ones, using a wood-fired oven *(forno a legna)*, usually open in the evenings only. Restaurant bills will usually include €1–3 per person for bread and cover charge *(pane e coperto)* and a 10–15 percent service charge. If service is not included it is normal to leave a tip. Some restaurants offer a set meal or *menu turistico*, which will be two or three courses with wine, service and cover included.

The prices indicated are a basic guide for a three-course evening meal per person excluding wine.

€€€€	over 45 euros
€€€	30–45 euros
€€	15–30 euros
€	below 15 euros

ALGHERO AND THE NORTHWEST

ALGHERO

Agriturismo Sa Mandra €€ *Strada Aeroporto Civile 21/a, tel: 0799 99150.* Book in advance for this *agriturismo*, 3km (2 miles) from Alghero's airport. Hearty Sardinian fare.

Caffè Latino € *Bastione della Madallena, tel: 0799 79330.* The attraction here is not so much food but the setting on the Maddalena bastion and the glorious sea views from the esplanade. Even off-season you may have to wait for a terrace table. No main meals, but snacks are available all day. The perfect spot for a predinner aperitif.

La Lepanto €€€ *Via Carlo Alberto 135, tel: 0799 79116.* The sea-view setting and the tempting display of fresh fish make this one of

Alghero's most sought-after restaurants. Lobster is served in a variety of ways and is especially memorable served with a mousse of ricotta, celery, parsley, basil and tomato. Closed Monday.

Al Tuguri €€€€ *Via Maiorca 113, tel: 0799 76772*. Alghero's most elegant restaurant, occupying two little rooms in an old mansion. Its reputation is based on fish, and the menu depends on the catch of the day. Typically it will include seabass, seabream, mullet and the full range of seafood, including lobster served in the Catalan or Aragonese style and sea urchins *(ricci del mare)* from November to April. A special meat-based menu ensures that carnivores are not ignored; there's a separate menu for vegetarians. Closed Sunday.

BOSA

Borgo Sant'Ignazio €€–€€€ *Via Sant'Ignazio 33, tel: 0785 374129*. Fresh fish and home-made pasta with seafood sauces are favourites at this enticing restaurant in the old town. Specialities are the clam and mussel soup, carpaccio of artichoke with smoked *bottarga* (mullet roe), black ravioli with cuttlefish and scampi sauce, and prawns with mushrooms, pepper and Malvasia wine. Closed Wednesday.

CASTELSARDO

Il Cormorano €€€ *Via Colombo 5, tel: 0794 70628*. Popular with visitors for its fish and seafood, cheerful décor and professional service. Pastas come with mussels, spiny lobster, cockles and sea urchins, and can be followed by smoked tuna or fresh mullet, bream, sole or lobster. Choose from around 300 different wines or go with the excellent *vino da casa* (house wine). Closed Tuesday off season.

SÁSSARI

L'Assassino €–€€ *Vicolo Ospizio Cappucini 1, tel: 0792 35041*. An atmospheric and very Sardinian trattoria hidden away near the pretty Piazza Tola. This is not a place for the squeamish. Typical dishes are pigs' trotters, donkey, sweetbreads, and sheep's entrails with peas – along with plenty of conventional meat dishes. Closed Wednesday.

STINTINO

Silvestrino €€€ *Via Sassari 14, tel: 0795 23007*. At this fish restaurant in the Hotel Silvestrino, a homely dining room and summer veranda are the setting for seafood risottos, lobster soup, *baci alla Silvestrino* (delicate pastries with spinach and ricotta) and *fregola sarda ai crostacei* (pasta with shellfish).

COSTA SMERALDA AND THE NORTHEAST

BAIA SARDINIA

Grazia Deledda €€€ *on the road to Cannigione, tel: 0789 98990*. One of the north's finer dining establishments, renowned for traditional fish-based Sardinian dishes. It's also a hotel with 11 comfortable rooms. Try *bottarga* (dried roe) of tuna, delicious home-made pastas with seafood, meat or mushroom sauces, and lobster Spanish-style. Open Easter to mid-October only.

CANNIGIONE

La Colti €–€€ *Strada Arzachena-Cannigione, tel: 0789 88440*. *Agriturismo* in rural Gallura serving locally grown organic vegetables, home-made soups and pastas, suckling pig and wild boar. All washed down with tumblers of local wine, followed by *seadas* (cheeses pastries with honey) and a glass of *mirto* (myrtle liqueur) on the house.

OLBIA

Gallura €€€ *Corso Umberto 145, tel: 0789 24648*. Michelin-starred trattoria in the town centre, renowned in particular for fresh shellfish. The lengthy menu features delicious homemade pasta and 30 different types of risotto. Reservations advised. Closed Monday.

SANTA TERESA DI GALLURA

Canne al Vento €€ *Via Nazionale 23, tel: 0789 754219*. The unremarkable location, on the main road going into town, is compensated by attractive décor and professionally prepared authentic Gallurese specialities. Regional dishes come in hearty portions and include *gnocchi cirumedda*, hand-made gnocchi with tomato sauce, sheep's cheese and sausage, and *zuppa quatta* (more akin to a cheese pie than a soup), made with fresh and mature cheeses. July–Aug open evenings only. Closed Monday off season.

La Torre €€ *Via del Mare 36, tel: 0789 754600.* Named after the nearby Spanish watchtower, and popular for fresh seafood, pasta and the pleasant setting above the main beach. Try *malloredus alla Torre* (shell-shaped pasta with cream, mushrooms and tomatoes), *penna alla Gallurese* (pasta with aubergine, peppers and tomatoes) or *arselle alla marinara* (pasta with seafood) and follow with seabass, gilt head bream, squid or lobster. Closed Wednesday off season.

NUORO AND THE EAST

DORGALI

Ristorante Ispinigoli €€ *Grotta di Ispinigoli, Dorgoli, tel: 0784 95268.* This capacious restaurant serves fish and spit roasts to tourists visiting the stunning Ispinigoli caves across the road. The panoramic dining area overlooks craggy hills, with the Gulf of Orosei visible in the far distance.

NUORO

Canne al Vento €€ *Viale Repubblica 66, tel: 0784 201762.* The menu concentrates on traditional Barbagia fare: *prosciutto* from Olieno, suckling pig, wild boar and horse, served with fresh local vegetables. A characteristic regional starter is *pane frattau* (crisp sheets of bread served with tomato sauce, eggs and pecorino cheese). Don't miss out on the delicious Sardinian desserts, and notably the *sebadas* (fried ricotta-filled pastries with honey). Closed Sunday.

Su Nugoresu € *Piazza San Giovanni 7, tel: 0784 258017.* Simple and homely little trattoria pizzeria on the central piazza, specialising in typical fish and meat of the region.

OLIENA

Su Gologone €€€ *Località Su Gologone, Oliena, tel: 0784 287668.* In the wild Sopramonte hill country, the Su Gologone has been renowned since 1960 for its country cuisine. It is also a hotel with 65 rooms so reservations are essential. Suckling pig, goat and lamb roast on spits in the huge fireplace while guests tuck into smoked hams, salamis, cheeses and home-made pastas. For those with a hearty appetite, the taster menu is the best way to try all the specialities. The flower-decked terrace, overlooking the hills, is a lovely spot to dine. Closed October to mid-March.

ORISTANO AND THE WEST

CABRAS

Il Caminetto €€ *Via Battisti 8, tel: 0783 391139.* Large, smart restaurant in the centre of Cabras serving mullet from the nearby lagoon. You can have it either simply grilled, salted and cooked in herbs, or flavouring spaghetti in its sundried roe form *(spaghetti alla bottarga).* Closed Monday except August.

ORISTANO

Craf €€€ *Via de Castro 34, tel: 0783 70669.* A convivial trattoria with brick vaults and old photographs of Oristano. This is a good place to try the island's specialities, whether it's Sardinian pasta dishes, gilthead bass cooked in the local Vernaccia wine, wild boar or – less likely to appeal to tourists but quite tender and tasty – *asinello in padella ai funghi* (donkey cooked with mushrooms). Meals are usually rounded off with a small glass of Vernaccia. Closed Sunday.

Da Gino €€ *Via Tirso, 13, tel: 0783 71428.* This central, family-run trattoria is a good bet for local dishes such as *spaghetti ai ricci* (with sea urchins) and *tagliattelle con carciofi e bottarga* (with artichokes and mullet roe) or push the boat out and opt for Gino's lobster. Closed Sunday.

Antica Hostaria €€€ *Via Cavour 60, tel: 0706 65870*. A long-established restaurant with an elegant, intimate setting. Fresh flowers grace the tables and the pink walls are packed with paintings by the owner's brother. The chef's recommendations change every other day but you can expect to find delicious pastas with seafood or meat sauces, carefully prepared fresh fish dishes and some fine Sardinian wines. Closed Sunday.

Dal Corsaro €€€€ *Viale Regina Margherita 28, tel: 0706 64318*. Save this for a special occasion. It's among the finest restaurants on the island, serving exquisite dishes in very formal, elegant surroundings. The specialities are mainly fish-based and include mussel and clam soup, baby squid stuffed with cheese, lobster salad and fillet of bass with saffron.

Italia €€€ *Via Sardegna 30, tel: 0706 57987*. One of the oldest restaurants in town, established (on the other side of the road) in 1921 and run by the Mundula family ever since. Customers are welcomed with an aperitif, then can choose between the 'bistro' downstairs or the slightly more elegant and expensive upstairs restaurant. Typical dishes here are seafood *antipasti*, fish soup, *fregola con arselle* (couscous-type pasta with clams) and spit-roast pork. Closed Sunday.

Lilliccu €€ *Via Sardegna 78, tel: 0706 52970*. Not one of the most conspicuous trattorias along Via Sardegna with its dark exterior and net curtains. But emphasis here is on food rather than setting; it was established 80 years ago, and locals flock here for the professionally prepared fish dishes and Sardinian specialities at affordable prices. The fish soup is legendary; it's normally served on Tuesday and Friday and should be ordered in advance.

VILLASIMIUS

Stella d'Oro €€ *Via Vittorio Emanuele 21, tel: 0707 91255*. One of the first restaurants in the region, founded in 1926. The German novelist Ernst Jünger was the first visitor to stay here when it became a hotel in the 1950s. It is a family-run, unpretentious place with a delightful courtyard and central fountain for *al fresco* dining. Among the favourite dishes are *malfatti* (ricotta with spinach) and, to order in advance, fish soup and lobster.

THE SOUTHWEST

CAPOTERRA

Sa Cardiga e Su Schironi €€–€€€ *Località Maddalena Spiaggia, 10km (6 miles) southwest of Cágliari, tel: 0707 1652.* Set in an unprepossessing area on the coast between Cágliari and Pula, this is arguably the best value seafood restaurant on the island. It's a huge place, usually full of locals and popular for weddings and parties. A wonderful array of fish and seafood are displayed in a boat inside the restaurant. Closed Monday.

IGLÉSIAS

Gazebo Medioevale €€ *Via Musio 21, tel: 0781 30871.* Atmospheric restaurant in the old town of Iglésias with medieval brick arches and masks on the walls. Fish predominates and varies according to the market. The favourite dessert is a home-made *semi-freddo*. Closed Sunday.

ISOLA DI SAN PIETRO

Dau Bobba €€€ *Lungocanale delle Saline, just west of Carloforte, tel: 0781 854037.* Inconspicuous location overlooking the saltpans and flamingoes on the outskirts of Carloforte, but worth a detour for Chef Giorgio's wonderful tuna dishes, pasta sauces and choice of wines. He uses every part of the tuna and serves it in a remarkable variety of ways. Vegetables are a cut above average, being all home-grown. The restaurant was converted from an old tuna fishing factory and named after Bobba, one of the fishermen who worked here. The courtyard is delightful location to dine during the summer months.

INDEX

Berlitz® pocket guide

Sardinia

Second Edition 2008

Written by Susie Boulton
Principal photographer: Chris Godet
Series Editor: Tony Halliday

Photography credits
All pictures by Chris Godet, except page 37 by Marco Casiraghi/Alamy, page 44 by Bruno Morandi/Powerstock, page 59 by Gregory Wrona, page 62 by 4Corners Images/Ripani Massimo

Cover picture: M.L. Sinibaldi/Corbis

No part of this book may be reproduced, stored in a retrieval system or transmitted in any form or means electronic, mechanical, photocopying, recording or otherwise, without prior written permission from Berlitz Publishing. Brief text quotations with use of photographs are exempted for book review purposes only.

All Rights Reserved
© 2008 Berlitz Publishing/Apa Publications GmbH & Co. Verlag KG, Singapore Branch, Singapore

Printed in Singapore by Insight Print Services (Pte) Ltd, 38 Joo Koon Road, Singapore 628990. Tel: (65) 6865-1600. Fax: (65) 6861-6438

Berlitz Trademark Reg. U.S. Patent Office and other countries. Marca Registrada

Every effort has been made to provide accurate information in this publication, but changes are inevitable. The publisher cannot be responsible for any resulting loss, inconvenience or injury.

Contact us

At Berlitz we strive to keep our guides as accurate and up to date as possible, but if you find anything that has changed, or if you have any suggestions on ways to improve this guide, then we would be delighted to hear from you.

Berlitz Publishing, PO Box 7910, London SE1 1WE, England.
fax: (44) 20 7403 0290
email: berlitz@apaguide.co.uk
www.berlitzpublishing.com